HOW TOP ENTREPRENEURS LEAD IN BUSINESS AND IN LIFE

Alinka Rutkowska | A'sha Love | Dr. Aby Lilian Mamboleo | Alexis Zen
Alina Okun | Beth Jannery | Brett Currier | Chris Roberts
Eric McDermott | Fadwa AlBawardi | Gennady Feller | Dr. Glen Robison
Johnny Marines | Kumar Parakala | Lance Graulich | Louis Columbus
Martin Rowinski | Megan Hightower Martins | Monah Al Jneibi
Nicolette Freeman | Per Sjöfors | Pippa Isbell | Dr. Prasad Kodukula
Rick Yvanovich | Sharon Lynn Wyeth | Stephanie Crowe

Published in the United States by Leaders Press.
www.leaderspress.com

ISBN **978-1-63735-190-1** (pbk)
ISBN **978-1-63735-201-4** (Amazon pbk)
ISBN **978-1-63735-191-8** (ebook)

SIMON & SCHUSTER

Print Book Distributed by Simon & Schuster
1230 Avenue of the Americas
New York, NY 10020

TABLE OF CONTENTS

Part 3: Mindsets 133

Part 4: Forward 207

INTRODUCTION

Have you ever wondered what characteristics set leaders apart from others? Is it just the fact that they are in charge, or is it something more fundamental? To dig a bit deeper, we could ask the question: "What makes successful leaders different from those who are less successful?" Another way to get at this same idea might be to ask the following: "What does it take to be a luminary leader?"

Luminary Leadership provides a variety of answers to these questions by combining the knowledge of a group of authors who have spent decades, in some cases whole careers, either delivering such leadership or studying it and teaching others how they can use it to improve their ability to lead.

Given the many challenges business leaders—and leaders in general—have encountered in recent years, the concept of leadership has undergone intense examination. With society forced to navigate a major pandemic, war, supply shortages, inflation, and natural disasters, there has been a tremendous need for luminary leaders to step up and do what great leaders do—help people, organizations, and society as a whole deal with, and overcome, the issues we face.

It is not so much that these challenges are unprecedented; it is that businesses today are being forced to deal with all, or many of them, at once, making it difficult for organizations to overcome them by simply continuing to do what they have been doing. When the hurdles to doing business as usual are so high, by-the-numbers, uninspired leadership can fall short. It's not that the old leadership principles don't apply—it's that given the scope of the issues many businesses face, they often must be updated to meet current conditions or combined with new ideas and techniques for maximum impact.

To help leaders rise above the many obstacles that can trip them up in today's complex business environment, the authors featured in *Luminary Leadership* draw on the extensive pool of experience and knowledge they have developed to detail the type of leadership that can create order out of chaos and help people and organizations overcome their greatest challenges. Taken together, these authors possess the collective knowledge to provide today's leaders with the strategies and techniques they need to help them motivate team members, learn from past mistakes, establish and communicate their vision, and achieve personal and organizational objectives.

One definition of a luminary leader is one who has overcome the challenges they have faced, learned from them, and made it through to the other side with their values and team intact. These leaders become stronger from such experiences, and they use this strength and the wisdom they have gained from effectively dealing with adversity to teach others how they can do the same.

During tumultuous times, it can be especially beneficial to hear from a wide variety of luminary leaders—leaders who have stood the test of time and risen to the top of their field—and learn about the strategies and tactics such leaders use to inspire others and achieve their goals.

Focusing on the approach they take offers insight not just into leadership as it relates to a particular sector or industry but also to the idea of leadership itself—what it means to be a leader and how leaders can use their position to improve their organization and the lives of those around them.

Each of the authors featured in this book have compressed their most impactful ideas about luminary leadership into a chapter's worth of observations about what makes great leadership. In these chapters, the authors distill their thoughts, which were developed over the course of their varied careers, on luminary leadership in the form of vignettes, anecdotes, lessons, guidelines, and insights about what it means to be a leader today and how leaders can learn to develop their approach, improve their skills, live their values, and achieve their success. The authors cover a wide variety of leadership approaches and describe related techniques and tactics, providing a truly comprehensive view of what luminary leadership means.

The featured authors run the gamut of leadership expertise and experience, from the frontlines of corporate America to the halls of academia, from domestic and international consulting to the heights of the entertainment industry, from consulting for consultants to leading digital transformations and much more. The body of knowledge they possess as a whole is truly astounding—and just as important is their ability to clearly explain how you can put the principles they have learned into effect in your own leadership efforts.

While each chapter contains a thorough account of what it takes to be a luminary leader from the author's perspective, the general approach they take to covering the topic can be categorized as follows:

- Beginnings: Authors who focus on how incidents in their youth formed their leadership style
- Teaming: Authors who focus on how leadership can help increase the productivity and motivation of a team
- Mindsets: Authors who focus on having the right mental approach to leadership
- Forward: Authors who focus on how leadership can provide needed changes as we move ahead

Whether your interest is to learn more about modern leadership approaches or to adopt those you find most compelling for yourself, *Luminary Leadership* offers an in-depth look into the traits, values, and practices of successful leaders. In digging into the nitty-gritty of what it takes to deliver luminary leadership in the modern business landscape, the book offers a firsthand look at how the advanced leadership techniques underlying such leadership are being used today.

PART ONE:

BEGINNINGS

Lessons that shaped a leader's young life

Pivoting and Persisting in Life and Leadership

Alinka Rutkowska

Alinka Rutkowska is the CEO of Leaders Press a USA Today *and* Wall Street Journal *bestselling press, where she helps entrepreneurs create books from scratch and then launches them to bestseller status with a 100 percent success rate.*

She has helped more than 172 authors get on the USA Today *and* Wall Street Journal *bestseller lists. Her mission is to help 10,000 entrepreneurs share their wisdom with the world by 2030.*

Alinka is an official member of the Forbes Business Council, and her cutting-edge book creation process has been featured in Entrepreneur *magazine.*

To learn more about Alinka, Leaders Press, and how this anthology and many of the solo books of the entrepreneurs featured here were created, visit http://www.leaderspress.com.

Youthful Leadership

Have you ever watched youngsters and thought, "I see the entrepreneurial spirit in them?"

Well, I believe I demonstrated some leadership qualities when I was young. I created my first business when I was in elementary school. I would buy these big bags of M&M's and divide them into small bags of M&M's and sell them to my friends, with a really good margin.

When I was a bit older, probably ten or eleven years old, there was a school newspaper that I didn't like very much. I thought, "Maybe we can give them some competition." So I created this competing school newspaper and wrote all the articles for it. Once that first issue came out, people started asking, "Can I contribute something?" I thought, "Wow, I can actually lead this whole effort. I don't have to do it myself." That was, I think, my first team, and I started putting this newspaper together, getting other kids to write stuff for it. I actually didn't have to do a lot of work, in terms of the content, just more of the organizational stuff of getting it out.

The first official leadership role I had was again at school. I was maybe thirteen or fourteen. I was elected president of the class. I don't even remember what the responsibilities were. But I remember there were a lot of behind-the-scenes things that I had to deal with that others had no idea about. It gave me an idea of all the extra work and responsibilities you have as a leader that aren't even on people's radar and probably don't get acknowledged.

Corporate Drone to Entrepreneur

To climb the corporate ladder or become an entrepreneur—is that the question?

Initially, my idea for a career goal was to climb the corporate ladder. I did that for three years. I worked at Shell and Whirlpool. I started as a marketing assistant at Shell and then moved on to Whirlpool, where I was part of the Fast Track program, which was meant to shape their future leaders. This involved three projects in three different areas: logistics, manufacturing, and customer service. Then, after completing that training program, my first job was in operations.

This was a huge company, and after the initial excitement of "Wow, I'm working at this well-known place," after this honeymoon period, where you only see the positives, I started seeing all the rest. One of the things that bothered me was that my decision-making power was very small. I was assigned to a confined area where I had little wiggle room to make any decisions or do anything. I felt I had much more potential than the role offered. I just started feeling that there was more out there for me. It was a long process of self-realization, but eventually, I made the decision to do something else.

I think entrepreneurship is a great way to learn and grow as a leader, because you start it by yourself, and you need to have some sort of vision that you believe in and then work on transferring that enthusiasm to others. You're a leader if you have followers, and you'll have followers if you first create something or at least have a dream that others believe in as well. I would say my leadership role started not when I turned into a solo entrepreneur or founded Leaders Press but when I hired the first person, because then I became a true leader and had someone buying into my vision.

The Challenge of Growth

How do you transmit culture as the company grows? My biggest struggle as a leader is probably right now, when we have almost forty people at Leaders Press. I have very little contact with the majority of the people who work here, so it's only the people I work closest with whom I'm able to know well. It's important to me to strive to understand what's driving them, what their dreams are, and how everything can be synced so that their dreams are part of my dream. The further away I am from people on the team, the less of that connection there is.

The objective is to have this enthusiasm and culture spread all over the organization. We'll only be getting bigger because we have many opportunities to grow. So when we double or triple the people here, that will be even more of a challenge.

Looking back on when I worked at large corporations, I realized I had no connection with the top leadership there at all. That feeling of disconnection is understandable because it's impossible with thousands or tens of thousands of employees, but some elements of the culture were still conveyed. For us, the challenge is to have people following the vision and rowing the boat in the same direction while we're growing, and I as the leader have less communication with everybody.

Leadership Style and Motivation

How should motivating people influence your leadership style?

In terms of leadership style, somebody said that I'm a leader from behind. I don't know if that's accurate, but I do like to work with people who are leaders themselves, who take responsibility for their own lane, and who don't necessarily need to be given a ton of motivation. The way I want to lead is really by asking questions, using the Socratic method, if you will. If we have certain goals, and they are not being met, we need to ask the questions that will get us there. "Why is it that way?" etc. If we ask the five whys, we're probably going to get to the core, the real reason why something is happening or not happening.

I also try to understand what motivates people, because not everybody is motivated by money. People value different things: freedom, free time, flexibility, creativity, decision-making ability, etc. I think you should only have as many people directly reporting to you as you can understand, and knowing what motivates them is crucial to understanding them.

The people I work with the closest are all different and really don't need to be motivated by me at all, because they're self-motivated. The ideal people I like to work with are the ones I don't need to point my finger at and tell, "Do this, do that," but rather, they raise their hand and say, "I see an opportunity here. Why don't we do this?" Or, "I see a threat here. How about we defend ourselves by doing this?"

The Qualities of a Leader

What does it mean to be a leader?

I think the values a leader has should center on having respectful relationships based on qualities such as trustworthiness, openness, and confidentiality. It's important to be in sync—a true leader is only a leader if they have followers, so they have to be able to convey their vision. Also, not being a jerk—being in a leadership position doesn't authorize you to be rude. You should treat everybody with respect.

For a leader or anyone, I really believe in constant learning and lifelong learning. I belong to a bunch of masterminds, which are groups designed for leaders or entrepreneurs only. If you hang out with people like that, you're able to talk about any problems you might have or challenges with your team or with your business vision. It's really great to be able to get feedback from somebody in a similar position—to have this peer-to-peer connection.

Becoming a Better Leader

How can you continue to improve your leadership skills?

You need to be coachable, to continue growing as a leader, and to understand that just because you've arrived here doesn't mean you're going to grow 5x or 10x. To take that next step, you may need outside help, either in the form of a consultant or by bringing in somebody senior to help you grow. Otherwise, you won't be able to grow the business and lead as effectively as it gets larger.

I had the two key people on the operations team go through a course for COOs. As I see it, maybe 80 percent of all business is the same, with just 20 percent that is different. Why reinvent the wheel if there's already a standard operating procedure you can use?

I find lifestyle pursuits can be analogous to what you're doing in business. I ride horses, and I see so many metaphors or concepts I can take from there. While I talk about horses, I'm sure people could use any other topic that they're passionate about for the same purpose. For example, like with horse riding, you may need to jump through obstacles (and there will always be obstacles to jump through). First of all, to learn how to do it, you have to exercise patience and realize that you're not going to get a horse from not jumping to jumping in the Olympics overnight.

It's step-by-step-by-step. Every day is a win, or sometimes not, but you make progress every day, especially if you keep your eyes on the prize. You have your goal, and you keep going. To be able to appreciate it, you have to realize that the sweat is part of the process.

Soft Skills and Leadership

Have you ever wondered about skills a leader needs to know but usually aren't taught in school?

In terms of leadership skills, it's important to be able to communicate how you are going to lead and communicate with people with empathy—to understand them by engaging in active listening. It's imperative to talk to people in a way that they feel heard, and you can convey what you really mean. These are all soft skills, essentially, and almost none of them are taught at school, which I find quite interesting.

I developed these skills mostly through experience. I did study negotiations at university, but I look at that as a bonus. Some of these things you will learn if you study a bit of psychology, which I did as well. But for a lot of them, you really need to either learn from books or through some other training or experience. These soft skills are vital if you want to be a leader who people will follow.

Leadership Success (and Failure)

Is it really failure if you learn from it?

Measuring success as a leader depends on people's goals. To me, a major measure of success is turnover. How many people want to stay, and how many want to go, and after what period of time? This turnover rate is a number you know—it's not an opinion. Numbers don't lie. That's why being empathetic is important, but so is looking at the numbers, because they will tell you what's really going on.

I think another marker of success as a leader is that people don't abandon you even when things are not looking great. They understand your vision and know that life is composed of ups and downs, and they stick with you either way.

Failure as a leader is not that everything you've been working to achieve doesn't happen, or the business fails or had to file for bankruptcy, because those are actually learning experiences. You can take all that and create something else and bring in another team and still be a leader.

I think failure is giving up.

If I had the chance to do it again, I would probably get mentorship earlier. When you first get started, you usually have a small budget or are bootstrapped and look at everything as an expense. But it's important to start having the mindset of looking at things as an investment and having a mentor or somebody working on the team who can help bring results that you will never be able to achieve yourself.

Also, learning how to hire is key. Knowing what questions to ask and how to evaluate the person that you're interviewing is super important, because if you don't do it right away, it costs more in terms of finances, time, and emotional investment if you make the wrong hire and then have to let them go.

Enjoy the Ride

How will you know you are successful if you don't celebrate it?

It's very important to enjoy the ride and to celebrate successes, even if they seem small, because once we achieve one goal, we often go right after the next one without even acknowledging what we just did. A good exercise is to say,

"Okay, look at where we are now. Where's the business now?" or, "Where am I personally now? And where were we three years ago? Did we ever think where we are today could have been possible?"

Probably not. So just acknowledge that and say, "Okay, wow, three years ago, I was nowhere near where I am now." And I think that's a really good way to measure success rather than always looking towards the future, at a distant horizon that's a moving target. Instead of never being satisfied, look back and see how much you've achieved in the last three years, or whatever period of time you've determined that's adequate, and celebrate that.

Shining a Light on Leadership

Pippa Isbell

Pippa Isbell helps leaders do their best work through the coaching, learning and development she facilitates.

A qualified trainer, she also has an Advanced Practitioner Diploma in Executive Coaching awarded by the Academy of Executive Coaching. She believes coaching is about transformation. Whether in small steps over time or a major breakthrough, seemingly achieved in an instant, it is about achieving sustainable change.

Pippa has extensive experience as a professional speaker. Drawing on her business background, she brings a blend of entrepreneurial insight, business acumen, and a practical approach to the workshops and courses she runs. She uses energy, humor, and storytelling skills to engage audiences and deliver messages which resonate.

Her areas of expertise include leadership, presence and influence, emotional intelligence, motivation, gender diversity and inclusion, storytelling, and presentation skills.

She has a business background in leisure and hospitality. She founded, built, and sold her own public relations consultancy, was a partner in a hotel investment and asset management company, served as Chief Executive of an international public relations and digital consultancy, and was Vice President responsible for global corporate and investor communications at Orient-Express Hotels, now Belmond.

To learn more about her work, visit www.pivotality.com.

Early Days

As a leader, it was not an auspicious start. I was a timid child, with a much more outgoing younger sister. I always pushed her forward, content to stand back. We were a military family, so my early life was all about change. We moved to new towns and even countries on a regular basis. At twelve, I was sent to an English boarding school. That is when I aspired to be a ringleader, one of the girls who set the agenda. That experience combined with my ambition, built my resilience. Over time, I started to push myself forward. I became an early adopter of the 'feel the fear and do it anyway' philosophy.

In my first job, as a member of the training department in a world-famous department store, I found myself teaching groups of new trainees. I developed a system of forgetting an important item at the beginning of each class so that I could leave the room to calm my nerves. Fortunately, others saw more in me than I did myself and offered stretch opportunities from which I discovered more inner courage than I realised. I learned by doing, and my confidence developed along the way.

Carpe Diem and Hang On Tight

In life, we never know what is around the corner. At the start of my career, opportunities came my way, and I took them, but I can't honestly say that I had a career plan or particular goals. But at age twenty-six, I had huge luck, I had the huge luck of working for an incredibly charismatic leader who ran an educational charity. On his team, I went from "having a job" to wanting a career. Having a demanding boss who made work both fun and significant, who challenged me and believed in me, and senior colleagues who were great role models was the making of me.

The path took twists and turns. I was promoted to Head of Publicity for the organisation. As a charity, every department, even one that would normally be a cost centre such as PR, had to make a profit. It was the best possible business training. We had to earn every penny we needed to spend, and a bit more. The way we did it was to create income streams not only from obvious subjects such as media training but also from a campaign to advance women in business, a passion of mine to this day.

I joined the Association of British Travel Agents as Head of Public Affairs. Over some years, I became a travel industry specialist. Though I would not have predicted this career turn, I stayed in this field for the next part of my career. In that role, I dealt with many PR consultancies and developed an ambition to start my own business, which I ran successfully for twelve years before selling it to a multinational consultancy.

I was headhunted to join an international hospitality group, Orient-Express Hotels, better known for its world-famous train than its collection of luxury hotels. During my time there, the organization grew to fifty businesses on five continents, and we took it public on the New York Stock Exchange. I could not have envisaged any of these opportunities when I started out, so my advice to everyone is this: keep an open mind. Work out your purpose, and follow that as every opportunity comes your way. My purpose was always about people, helping them grow and develop, whatever the mission of the team I was leading. Eventually, that led me back to my roots in people development, business coaching, and leadership training.

Climbing the Mountain

My very first leadership role came with a challenge. I inherited a team where I was the youngest person. Unbeknownst to me, one of the senior managers in the department had applied for my job, and her sister worked with us too. I had two ready-made obstacles sitting across the floor from me from day one. I had to win them over, or I would have lost everyone. I had a terrific mentor who ran another division, and his objective and robust advice was invaluable. I learned to let the sisters get on with their own field of expertise and rely on their advice. I learned not to give up in the face of the initial hostility and to work on uniting the whole team.

In my own business, I learned that the volume of work and the weight of responsibility of employing people was exhausting and sometimes overwhelming. I had to learn to take care of my own well-being to be able to do my job. I learned the hard way to focus on the 20 percent of tasks that delivered 80 percent impact.

Being a Leader

Being a leader is all about what you do. The context of leadership is continuously evolving, so your style and focus will need to flex as times change along with team members' expectations. Everyone is there for the same purpose, so they need to understand the vision of the organisation and how they can contribute. The role of the leader is to make sure everyone knows what the task is and how they can play their part.

Team culture is vitally important, and that comes from the leader too. People perform best in an atmosphere of trust and support. That comes from being fair, open, and loyal. I used to tell my team members that they would never get into trouble with me for making mistakes or reaching too far, but woe betide them if I had to hear about it from someone else.

Whenever you can, create opportunities for your people. A young woman joined my team to provide administrative support, but we soon noticed that not only was she incredibly efficient, she also had a real way with people. She made connections and grew in confidence, so we promoted her into an executive role, and eventually, she managed one of our workstreams. Supporting and nurturing people is incredibly rewarding for both parties.

Motivating people is an ongoing challenge. As a leader, I try to get to know individuals as rounded beings. Beyond the job they do on my team, what makes them tick? What are their skills, views, and interests? How can I give them the opportunity to do what they want to do and grow while achieving the task? I'm always looking for opportunities and encouraging them to do the same. They are responsible for their own career progression, but I'm the team coach, and I want us all to win together.

Acknowledging success is so important. I treasure notes of thanks or commendation received from my bosses and clients—and even my team members—over the years. I'm proud to be mentioned in a shout-out or if people say they enjoy working with me. I want to motivate others by giving that same reward and creating a culture in my team where we all applaud achievement, however big or small.

Leaders need to celebrate what people are good at, have their backs when things go wrong, stretch them so they develop new skills, and encourage everyone to keep learning. And very importantly, have fun along the way. That's what builds a community.

Leadership styles are grounded in personal values, so it's important to know what yours are and how they show up. For me, some of the most important are honesty and integrity, fairness, and loyalty. I also value being genuine and trustworthy and being a good and consistent communicator.

I was lucky enough to work for several excellent leaders during my career. They taught me the importance of knowing and sticking to your values and the pain of compromising them. I watched what worked and learned from what did not. I learned from leaders who were crystal clear about the task, visionaries embarking on something new, campaigners who wanted to change the way things were done, industry leaders, and experts. Each of them changed my view of how to lead in some way, and I'm incredibly grateful to them all. I still practice what they taught me.

Continuing to Grow

People talk about keeping current. I want to do that too but also continue to stretch myself and my leadership practice by learning, ideally something new every day. I try to set aside time to read business articles, listen to podcasts, watch TED talks, and take courses when I can. I am curious about what is coming over the horizon, both in general terms and within my discipline.

It's also important to reach outwards—to network and make connections with people. Every interaction offers opportunities to broaden your own perspective.

And it's a responsibility of leadership to pay it forward—to respond to the help and support you had on your career path by offering the same to others coming up the ladder behind you. There are lots of smart people who may not have had the opportunities we've had. It's our job to help them grow.

Leadership Essentials

Over many years of working with leaders at all levels, I've come to recognise what sets everyday managers apart from actual leaders: it's a mix of personality traits, natural behaviours, and learned skills. Among the skills that can be learned are how to develop a vision for what you want to achieve and create a strategic plan to get there. Communication skills can also be learned and honed into storytelling that convinces your audience. It goes without saying that you need to have a command of the numbers and data that determine performance.

It helps if you are an open person with the ability to earn trust and the confidence to take people along with you. Research has shown that along with belonging to a community, people want to understand the significance of their work. However small a cog, however big the engine, they want to know their work contributes to the success of the whole. There is a lot of talk about authenticity and vulnerability as a leader, and to me, that simply means being your genuine self and having the courage to let that show and fight your corner.

Successful leaders have the task nailed down: they are interested in people and communicate instinctively and empathetically with the individuals who make up their team. They put effort into helping them develop and grow and take the next step in their careers, even if it means losing a valuable team member to an unmissable opportunity.

And their people respond by uniting around the common purpose, supporting one another, and delivering great work.

Leaders have also developed the habit of reflection. They may keep a journal, but at the very least, they ask themselves two questions daily: what went well today and what could have gone better? Success is delivery against goals and objectives, with the whole team pulling together to achieve it. Failure on the other hand (barring serious disasters which rarely happen in reality) is an opportunity for critical thinking and great learning.

Onwards and Upwards

If I was transported back to the starting line, how would I run the race this time? I'm honestly not sure I'd do anything differently. I've learned so much along the way. I could have been a better academic student. Who knows what opportunities would have opened up with better grades? That's certainly advice I'd give my younger self—knuckle down, and give yourself the best launchpad. To others starting out on their leadership journey, I'd say believe in your own power. Have confidence that you've got this. Leadership is a lifelong challenge.

Do your very best every single day, and don't sweat the small stuff or dwell on what could have been. Learn, apply, adapt, go forward—and repeat. Above all, enjoy the ride!

Connect with Pippa Isbell at www.pivotality.com.

Qualities of a Developing Leader

Dr. Glen N. Robison

Dr. Glen N. Robison serves as Diplomate of the American Board of Multiple Specialties in Podiatry. He's board certified in Primary Care in Podiatric Medicine. Dr. Robison is a Jin Shin Jyutsu practitioner and certified Myopractor. He's the bestselling author of Healthy Dad Sick Dad: What Good Is Your Wealth If You Don't Have Your Health?[1] *and has been inducted into the prestigious Marquis Who's Who.*

Dr. Robinson leads his medical specialty in the use of Prolotherapy for stabilizing ankles, repairing torn ligaments and tendons, along with reducing bunions without surgery. He was a part of a medical mission to the Kingdom of Tonga.

Dr. Robison currently operates his private practice of twenty-two years in Mesa, Arizona, where he provides necessary services to his patients, both surgically and clinically. When Dr. Robison is not in clinic or writing books, he spends time studying and perfecting the Master of Art in oil painting.

---

[1] Glen N Robison, Healthy Dad Sick Dad: What Good Is Your Wealth If You Don't Have Your Health? (Carson City, NV: Lioncrest Publishing, 2021).

Bring Out the Leader in You

Over the years, I have observed that some people with great leadership qualities don't see themselves as leaders. I noticed that most of these individuals are not awakened to the qualities of leadership that already exist within themselves. It is my goal to help you identify the qualities of the great leader that already exist within you and, once you become aware of these attributes, set a course to confidently pursue your desires and dreams. The end results equate to being a leader in your field of expertise.

What are those qualities that I will discuss? Leaders learn to lead themselves first before leading someone else—they never quit, they don't let anyone steal their dreams, they stay persistent in their journey, they take satisfaction in accomplishment, they have a strong desire to always be learning something every day, and they are not afraid to change course or take a new direction even with all their training and expertise.

They also possess the following qualities: they dare to be different, they take the road less traveled, they see what others don't see, they always give thanks, and they point out other accomplishments, just to mention a few.

To help you understand those subtle qualities, I would like to take you on my journey that began at a young age, when I was told I would never make it into college. From that beginning, I've climbed up to my current status of operating a podiatric medical practice for over twenty-two years.

Sitting in my high school English class while staring outside the window—not even paying attention to what the teacher was saying—was a common routine of mine. If

I had written the daydreams that my mind took me to while observing the outside world, I would have made William Shakespeare—my first cousin twelve generations back—very proud of me. The difference between William and myself is fairly obvious: He is a heavily quoted author and a required read in most schools, while I, on the other hand, was just about to learn my fate when over the loudspeaker, a voice suddenly announced, "Glen Robison, could you report to the front office?" All I could think of now was, "Oh no, not again."

Saying No to What I Was Told and Listening to Myself Instead

As I proceeded down the long hallway and into the vice principal's office—who happened to be the high school counselor and the head coach of the football team, and who also was the most feared man on campus—I could sense that I was about to have a life-changing moment. This was one of those scariest moments in my life; I would have rather walked down a dark alley in the middle of the night alone than go see Coach Monsen. As I hesitantly approached his office, the secretary said, "Mr. Monsen, Glen is here to see you." I had no time to formulate a game plan on the what-ifs. As I stood there in his office, he looked at me and said, "No need to sit down, this will not take long," so I stood there at attention like I had just joined the military.

He did not bother to say, "How is your day?" or, "Do you know why you are here?" He just said, "Glen, you just got the lowest ACT score in the state of Utah and the fifth lowest percentile in the nation. Maybe you should go to vo-tech school or go and become a farmer like your dad. Good luck getting into college." The only thing that was going through my mind was, "What in the hell was vo-tech school?" And being a farmer like my dad was out of the question, because even the smell of dust or hay triggered my asthma attack. I didn't even dare ask what my score was, but the one thing that stood out in my mind was the phrase he had uttered: "Good luck getting into college." Those five words became the most powerful and profound words that I had ever heard. It was right then that I told myself, "Well, I will just retake the test my senior year and go to college."

My senior year came. I retook the test, and to my surprise, I got the same exact score. Most universities and colleges that I interviewed with either laughed at my score or told me the same thing my high school counselor said to me. I finally found a college that did not require any college examination to enter, and I was granted a leadership scholarship for being the senior class president and an officer in the FFA (Future Farmers of America).

Never Quit, Even if There's No Light at the End of the Tunnel

Things did not go well during my first quarter at college, and I lost my leadership scholarship because I did not keep my grades to the required level. Technically, I did not lose the scholarship, as I spent the scholarship money on the books required for my classes, so even though they said I lost my scholarship, it was already spent. Around this time, I started to believe what my high school counselor said to me, and so I took two years off from school.

After taking those two years off, I kept holding on to those five words: "Good luck getting into any college." I also held onto the words my mother said to me in front of my seven other brothers and sisters when I was young: "Glen is going to be the doctor in the family." I kept the hope inside alive no matter what I was told by anyone else.

So how did it end? There were many times when I had to give myself a time-out to catch my breath, but I never gave up on my long-term goal, which was to go as far as I could in academics, and when I got there, to go further. There was only one option in my mind in order to accomplish this, and that was to become a doctor.

I went back to college and graduated with an Associate Degree in Pre-Medicine. On the day of the graduation, I packed my car early that morning and walked over to the building where thousands of students in their caps and gowns were anxiously awaiting their diplomas. I did not walk with them because I knew I was not done. I had bigger things to do.

Don't Let Anyone Steal Your Dreams

To reach my dream of becoming a doctor, I had to go to a university and get my bachelor's degree. I was now a student at the same university that had once laughed at me when I got my ACT score.

I had been accepted into medical school and was just finishing my last semester when I got a notice from the university stating I needed a genetics class to graduate. This class was only offered the following year in the fall. Another setback? With this new requirement, I was forced to call the medical school that had accepted me and explain the situation. They said they needed to review this, and they would get back to me.

After crapping bricks for a few weeks, I received a letter stating that it was okay to start medical school in the fall. In those four years of medical school, nobody knew I only had an associate degree when everyone else had bachelor's and master's degrees from high-ranking universities.

Staying Persistent in Your Journey

Medical school came with many short-term goals, like passing each class each semester, and with the long-term goal of finishing medical school and graduating. To write all that I experienced during medical school would comprise volumes of books, so to keep it simple, I will say: medical school was brutal. Some of the insanely challenging experiences I faced included my living arrangement in the first year of school that forced me to sleep on a classmate's laundry room floor—and even at a bus stop—while I was trying to find a more permanent place to live.

Aside from the living situation, there was also a memorable experience of having my life threatened while walking to school, when a man approached me and told me that if I looked back, he would kill me.

An experience that happened in my junior year was the most memorable one. I had my vein injected with contrast dye so the radiologist could see a blocked kidney stone that had developed and was causing me excruciating pain. This resulted in an anaphylactic reaction. I stopped breathing and was near death. In the end, while this experience had set my health back over the years, it also gave me the awareness that something had to change with my health.

Taking Satisfaction in Accomplishment

The day I walked across the stage and received my diploma was a day that caused every event that I had gone through to be well worth it. Did I stop once I got my achievement? No.

After medical school, I went on to do a two-year surgical residency program. It was there that the chief of staff in my general surgery rotation—who also sat on the board at the medical school where I was doing my first-year residency program—offered for me to go to back medical school to become a general surgeon, but I turned it down. Instead, I was offered to go on a medical mission to the Kingdom of Tonga right out of my residency program. Loving what I do in my medical specialty, I jumped at this opportunity.

A Strong Desire to Always Learn Something New Every Day

In surgery, there is a saying "See one, do one, teach one." You first observe the surgeon on how they cut the skin within each layer, identifying vital structures along the way until you get to your intended purpose for the surgery. You fix the circumstance that caused you to go into surgery in the first place, and then you close each level as you leave.

Every step is vital and important. When you leave one step out, you can either cause unnecessary damage or unwanted complications. Once you have seen one surgery, then it is time to do one. You hold the surgical instruments and take instruction on each level of the surgery. Both steps may require multiple attempts to grasp the desired skill, but once you can do it in your sleep, you are now ready to teach one.

It Is OK to Adjust and Change Your Course at Times

I felt that some technique or studied discipline was missing within the first few years of my practice. I just felt I could offer more to my patients. So I studied the art of Myopractics and Jin Shin Jyutsu, becoming certified in both. I studied under the world-renowned prolotherapist Dr. Kent Pomeroy and learned of his amazing art of healing the body without surgery. This training has greatly benefitted hundreds of my patients over the years. Another way I have helped expand my practice is the subtle way of healing through color. After reading more about Andrea Moritz's healing power through colors, I took up oil painting and placed my finished artwork in my clinics. My latest area of study has been writing the bestselling book *Healthy Dad Sick Dad: What Good Is Your Wealth if You Don't Have Your Health?* That has been life-changing for my patients. The one principle I hold on to is to never stop learning and expanding your ability to serve and help those you are responsible for. The great thing about life is you never run out of something to learn and can constantly improve your skills.

A perfect example of a turning point in my career, which I mentioned in my book, *Healthy Dad Sick Dad*, was when my little girl just stopped eating for no apparent reason. I took her to specialists; the ER ran tests on her, and nobody could give me an answer as to why she was not eating. I made a phone call to a person who had helped me get out of trouble with my health and asked if he could look at her. Within minutes, he made a diagnosis and fixed the problem. Once I witnessed this, I had to know more, so I asked the question, "Will you teach me?"

Over the years, I have done fewer surgeries in the hospital and learned ways to help patients in a more natural or holistic way. For instance, reversing bunions without surgery or treating gout, diabetes, and toenail fungus with simple diets.

There will come a point in one's career—as it did mine—when the universe says, "I want to see if this person is ready for a change or a challenge." We don't have to ask for it. It just happens, and when it does happen, be open to it, because, at some point, you will look back and realize that all the time, money, and efforts molded you into a leader in your field just as it did for me. All you have to do is participate in the process.

Lead by Example

Looking back on my life, from when I was told I can't make it into college to now, it has been an incredible journey. I would not have changed anything along the way, both the good and the bad. Staying true to your dreams, desires, and aspirations of life will cause you to reflect on what I have reflected on while sharing my story—that I am a leader within my field and that my life was blessed with experiences and events that have shaped my character and developed me into the person I am today.

Identify your qualities, be patient but persistent in your journey, and always keep learning that one thing every day. Give thanks for your experiences, continue to lead by example, and don't let anyone at any time or any place steal your dreams. Wishing you much success!

So, You Want to Become a Consultant? How to Have a Career Awakening

Beth Jannery

Beth Jannery is Founder of Titan—www.titanstrategiccommunications.com—*a strategic communications consulting solutions company. Titan has two key offerings: consulting for clients in private and public sectors and Titan Consulting Certification for people who want to start their own consulting business.*

Prior to Titan, Beth served as Bureau Chief for Raytheon Technologies, a $64 billion-dollar multinational aerospace and defense conglomerate with 174,000 employees. She was Chief Marketing & Communications Officer and Senior Vice President for a billion-dollar company with 7,000 employees. Beth is a USA Today.

When I Grow Up

I grew up as a middle child living in a small southern Virginia town until we moved to New England the summer I turned nine. I spent carefree days chasing a feeling of freedom and was constantly curious. Anything felt possible.

During the day, I'd roam around barefoot exploring the neighborhood by cutting across fresh-cut and clover-filled lawns and peek into the lives of my neighbors. I'd run through sprinklers. I'd stop at the honeysuckle bushes and bury my head into the sweet scent and taste the floral nectar. On hot summer nights, I'd chase lightning bugs in the backyard.

Some mornings, I'd watch the milkman deliver glass bottles to a metal box that sat outside our front door. During the weeks we couldn't afford milk, I'd watch my mom scoop into a big red box from our hallway supply closet and stir a white substance called powdered milk into our water cups. I'd help in the garden by picking tomatoes or peas.

It was a simple and peaceful life, one that I crave today when life gets hectic. I always retreat to nature when I need to reflect, connect, decompress, and simply be still.

We had one car my father would drive to work at the local college where he was a music professor. I'd watch him leave in the morning from the front concrete step as he went out into the big world. I'd wonder what it would be like to one day work in the world. What would I do?

As he got into his white Chevy, he'd place his leather, rectangle briefcase filled with a metal coffee thermos onto the seat, shut the door, and drive off. These were the days before Starbucks drive-thru. I wondered where I'd go one day with my briefcase and coffee.

We Grow Up

Fast-forward: I would end up being a journalist who covered the Department of Defense. I'd be on the communications faculty of three different universities. I'd be a writer. I'd be a mom. I'd be an aerospace and defense company advisor. I'd be a thought leader. I'd be the founder of a consulting company. The key word is BE.

I'd simply be. To me, the act of being is a beautiful quality of a luminary leader. Being is the true nature or essence of a person. I believe that luminary leaders are people who understand how to tap into their true essence. They aren't afraid to show people who they are.

Back in southern Virginia, I was a deep thinker and had an analytical mind. I was an empath and an active listener. I was a problem solver who could walk into any room and assess the situation. I'd lay in bed falling asleep at night to the sound of crickets through the screen windows, and I'd dream of the big, wide world.

But the town felt too small for me. In the distance, I'd hear the train whistle blow. I'd fall asleep wondering about the world beyond my walls. It is a place and time I remember fondly, and I often visit it in my mind when I need to remember to be.

I'd often forget to be, and my search for something more would last for decades, until eventually, I learned to be more conscious in the present moment, align my values to my work, and create something from nothing. In other words, I'd learned to simply be. Be comfortable in my own skin. Be my authentic self. Be a risk taker.

We Become Consultants

A luminary leader is an authentic person who creates their own path in the world. I did it. And it was a career awakening. You can have one too. I believe anyone can create their own path. I believe we can all wake up to have a conscious career. One of the biggest risks I've ever taken was to go off on my own to create my own company, Titan. No matter what other work I do in life, I will always have Titan.

One day, I was walking in the woods, taking a quiet and solo sojourn, when a powerful idea came to me. It is in these quiet moments of being in nature where I get intuitive nudges from the universe. I always pay attention when this happens. It went like this: Now that I've figured out how to successfully become a consultant and start my own business, I can help others to do the same. I hear from so many people who say they wish they could create their own business and become a consultant, but they are afraid or don't know how.

I came up with a solution. I'll show them how. A new idea was born, called Titan Consulting Certification. It is a three-month process anyone can do from the privacy of their own home, on their own time. It is for anyone who is ready to make a change in their career.

Becoming certified as a consultant is a simple process, but one that is deeply challenging as it asks you to dive deep and dig into what you really want out of a career and out of life. It brings your skills and work goals into alignment with your values, to create a new offering for the world. I went through it and elevated my life, and now I have the opportunity to share it with others.

There are thousands of consultants and leaders out there, *by title only*. But not many that I would call conscious consultants. This certification elevates you to become a conscious consultant and business founder.

We Take Difficult Risks

Before anyone can make a change, they have a moment of clarity. Mine came when I was miserable. Waking up each day felt like the movie *Groundhog Day*, and I found myself in a 24/7 sleepwalk, doing it all over again the next day. My work life felt suffocating. I was going through the motions, not feeling inspired, going from paycheck to paycheck.

The great thing about suffering is when it gets too painful, we have an opportunity to change. Pay attention to that moment when your inner voice is hoarse from yelling out, *I can't take this anymore. I can't handle it anymore. This is not the life I am meant to live.*

That moment of suffering is the opportunity to change everything. The moment of surrender. The moment we decide on the possibility of living in the present moment. The moment we begin to explore being conscious.

That's what happened to me. I had a moment like that. The one where I let go of who I was and what I thought I should be doing, and everything changed. I chose the truest version of myself. I connected back to my authenticity and tapped into a greater consciousness. I remembered that little girl inside of me who once thought anything was possible.

I emerged with a new idea, a new business, and a new life. And so can you. It's like letting go of one trapeze swing and hanging in mid-air before you grasp onto the security of the next swing. That is the moment of letting go and entering into presence. Trusting. Awakening. Being.

And yes, we are still talking about work and careers. You can have this shift, too.

We Take the Titan Path

Taking the Titan Path means you chose your truest self. You chose work and people you love. And if you aren't even sure what that looks like, the process I developed helps to reveal it to you. That moment will come, if you allow it. You'll choose to be fully present and live, awakened. Or you'll opt to stay in the mundane cycle of the hypnotic and numb state of the daily grind of going through the motions, which is not living at all. If you are feeling the way I described, and you can relate to that miserable feeling, then it is time to get on the path to living fully present and conscious at work.

We Lead and Grow

Once you become a consultant and start your own business, you get to decide your leadership style. Before I started Titan, and got to lead the way I like, I struggled with my leadership style until I listened to my intuitive voice.

I was used to looking to Alpha types to give directions and pass on the decisions to the team. I began waiting for others to give me permission, even though inside I knew what I wanted to do. As a girl, I was taught to defer to men, or to my superiors, for guidance. But this mentality in a leadership role would only hold me back. I couldn't wait for others to approve my ideas. I had to trust my own power.

I overcame it when I embraced the nontraditional servant leader mindset. This means I align with a leadership style that embraces who I am naturally, someone who considers the well-being of those being served. Valuing and appreciating people for who they are, having humility, putting others first, and offering my trust to others feel like the right way for me to lead. I believe this is a form of luminary leadership.

Whenever I get a chance to ask leaders or mentors for advice, I jump at the chance to learn a new tool. Then I take the good and leave what doesn't resonate with me behind. So my advice to anyone wanting to become a consultant and start their own business is to stop playing small. Make a decision to live consciously and begin the journey toward doing what you enjoy and doing it with people you like. It's that simple.

Call to Action

Are you ready? Take the risk, inhale, smile, and join us at Titan to get certified as a consultant. Get ready to blow your own mind and become a conscious and luminary leader in the process.

You'll know you are ready for this change when the pain of staying the same gets too great.

Let's grow!

Enroll for Titan Consulting Certification at Learn more about Titan Certification at BethJannery.com or contact BethJannery@TitanStrategicCommunication.com.

The Path to Effective Leadership

Monah Al Jneibi

Monah Al Jneibi was raised in Abu Dhabi, United Arab Emirates (UAE), and holds a Master's Degree of Education Leadership. She has worked in the fields of Human Resources, Strategy Performance and Management and Knowledge Management for companies such as Royal Jet, Emirates Advanced Investments, Abu Dhabi Retirement, Pensions and Benefits Fund, and Emirates Nuclear Energy Corporation.

In 2011, she became the founder and owner of Quality for Life that provides management consultancy services. Through the company, Monah developed several knowledge-building projects, most notably the UAE National Games (UNG), the Art, Play, Learn Academy concept and Zayed's Galaxy (ZG).

Since 2012, Monah has been working on a unique project—one of its kind—the UAE National Games, which focuses on transferring knowledge between individuals and groups through physical, game-based learning. The games of the UNG have been conducted in several universities, organizations, and public events as a way to discover hidden talents in the audience.

Since 2017, Monah has worked on designing and developing a social networking application known as BFF Gram. This multifeatured social networking application will be known for its family/friends networking capabilities and is expected to launch in 2023.

Leadership Qualities: Where Do They Come From?

Leadership qualities can be sort of a tricky thing to grasp. On the one hand, we are all endowed with natural talents and skills that maybe others around us don't have. But that being said, these talents can take years to manifest in our lives, and even longer to hone, sharpen, and employ in our professional lives.

As a self-identified introvert, I definitely belong to the category of "Learned Leadership." It was initially very hard for me to take the reins and step into the spotlight, so to speak. As someone who is naturally quite shy, it was a big hurdle that I had to learn to overcome. For example, when I was much younger and still in school, I never found it difficult to assert myself as the leader when working in small groups with my peers. However, when it came to giving large presentations, or being up at the front of the classroom, I always blanched with fear. Thus, in my case, becoming a leader was more about unearthing my own leadership potential and allowing it to blossom, without attaching too much importance to the fear that was holding me back.

Dreams of Entrepreneurship

From a very young age, I was determined that I would become a successful entrepreneur. Unfortunately for me, my father had his own set of preconceptions about what my life should look like. Needless to say, in his imagination, those fantasies had a great deal more to do with law school than with an MBA program. From primary school until the moments leading up to my graduation, he never forgot to remind me of what "our" shared vision of the future was.

My father's dreams of me becoming a servant of the court, however, were dashed when he realized I would have to travel within the UAE for two hours to attend university classes. Although the education would have been free, it was ultimately my parents' cultural fear of a woman studying in another area of Abu Dhabi—particularly while alone—that was the price they were not willing to pay. I'd have to choose something else.

Yet, even as a child, I often carried around a notebook—a sort of ledger—filled with unrealized projects and businesses that I wanted to launch. Though I didn't have any working capital to speak of, I would write out detailed (and imagined) lists of expenses, busying myself with hypothetical payroll accounts, KPIs (key performance indicators), and quarterly goals I expected to hit. It was all in my imagination, but it nonetheless had a major impact on who I would become later in life.

With law school seemingly out of the question, and university looming ever closer on the horizon, I decided to put my dreams of entrepreneurial success aside for the time being in pursuit of a degree in education. It was, I felt, the only other area of interest that I could apply myself to. So I went through the motions and quietly completed the work I needed to do to earn my degree. Truth be told, I might have forgotten about my dreams for entrepreneurship entirely had it not been for a certain speaker who came to our university as I was nearing my graduation date.

I can't recall the occasion now, or even the speaker's name, but I have never forgotten the content of what he spoke about that day. From the front of the stage, he looked out into the audience and asked all of us to close our eyes. He asked us to imagine, with as much intensity and detail as we could muster, either a vision for how we wished our lives to be or else some concrete and tangible goal. "Hold it in your mind's eye," he told us. "Keep it there." Then he asked another question. While we were imagining this utopic scenario in our minds, he asked how old we saw ourselves to be. How old did we want to be when we achieved this personal vision of success? At the time, my 30s still seemed a long way off, so I picked the ripe old age of 35, figuring that would surely give me enough time to enact my vision.

The last question he asked us to answer was how much money did we envision having in our bank accounts by the time this vision unfolded for real. I settled for a clean and crisp 10 million U.S. dollars—shoot for the stars, right? By 35, I wanted to be a multimillionaire entrepreneur. That was the dream.

While I can't say that I have quite reached those pinnacles yet (I'm 40 now and actively still working on that 10 million), the exercise had a profound impact on how I would set my personal and professional goals in the future. In retrospect, it was the first time I was truly exposed to the power of visualizing my own success, and it reinvigorated me with fresh ideas of entrepreneurship, ideas that I would desperately need when I finally did start my own company.

Stepping Up to the Plate

My first real office of responsibility as a leader came about in 2011, when I opened my own consultancy business. As any founder or CEO can attest to, one of the initial challenges I faced was how to select the right people for my core team. I inherently understood that a company's success could be determined, in large part, by the congruency and overall "fit" of the internal culture. It wasn't just enough to hire talented people; I needed to instill in them a shared vision of our future if we were to be successful as a team. This certainly challenged my introverted nature, and I found that I had to really break free of my own restraints to step up as a leader. In my opinion, it's not enough just to be competent or good at your job when you're leading a company. You must also be able to inspire, motivate, and buoy the rest of your team up as well—and that kind of willpower takes time to develop.

One of the first projects that my team and I sought to introduce was a concept called the UAE National Games (UNG). The idea was rooted in my educational background, in that the main objective of the event was knowledge management (e.g., transferring knowledge from a myriad of experts to nonexperts/laypeople). The event was focused primarily on transferring knowledge from and to high school students and their respective skill sets. The event offered three types of games: educational (teaching students life skills like camping, interview techniques, fixing a car, etc.); entertainment (introducing new games like cup and card stacker, sand art, and more); and traditional (teaching children the traditions and customs of the country, such as building a boat or temporary "henna" tattoos). The idea was to bring in other entrepreneurs, expert coaches, speakers, and leaders from a diverse set of backgrounds to help sharpen the minds of the youth in an environment that was less formal than the classroom and more focused on game-based learning.

Ultimately, the event did not come to fruition, and I learned another invaluable lesson as an entrepreneur along the way: *capital is king*. Our vision was to enact the UAE

National Games by 2014, but we were unable to secure adequate funding from both private and government entities that were to sponsor the event. Thus, we were not able to achieve our vision. However, I do not consider the venture to be a total failure, not by a long shot. The secret to entrepreneurship, in my opinion, is not to strive so tirelessly to achieve perfection on the first try, but rather to be able to look at your "failures" with honesty and objectivity. So long as you can learn from your mistakes, on a long enough timeline, you will eventually succeed at what you set your mind to. The failure of the UAE National Games to take off was a hard pill to swallow, but as with any bump in the road, it was also an opportunity to pivot, reevaluate, and solidify my goals moving forward. Ultimately, I remain confident that this pivot will allow me to come back and make UNG a success in its next iteration—this time without the financial support of anyone else!

Your Leadership Style Will Change with You

In terms of leadership style, I would say that my personal journey has seen several evolutions and changes in the way I interact with team members. As with anything, you never want to be stagnant and stubborn in the face of change, especially when that change is innovation. However, two core characteristics that have remained throughout the years, and have been instrumental in my business leadership, would be *vision* and *democracy*.

I touched on this briefly earlier, but I cannot stress enough the importance of learning to communicate your vision as a leader. You can acquire all the talent, resources, and know-how you like to build your A-team from the ground up, but if you can't connect those individuals with a unified vision of the future, you're far less likely to ever achieve the results you desire. A good leader should not only act as the captain of the ship—navigating through sometimes treacherous waters—but he or she should also be able to articulate the destination to which the team is headed clearly and concisely. As a passionate leader, I try to bring an attitude of optimism, fortitude, and even playfulness to my team. There will be moments along the way that are more difficult than others, but it's important, I believe, for the leader to stay ever alert to their team's morale.

Once you have the engagement, once everyone is onboard and excited about the vision, it becomes a question of motivation. How do you motivate your team? One way is by allowing their strengths to shine! Back in 2011, when I was crafting my own team, I paid very special attention to making sure that everyone was in their "correct seat." For example, one of our team members had a very strong background in IT. Naturally, I wanted to give her an opportunity to showcase her skillsets, so I immediately assigned her to the technical challenges we were facing in our development. Another team member was an especially adept content creator, so we tasked her with the marketing, branding, and copywriting that we needed to generate awareness around the National Games.

The point here is that vision does not stop at the macro level. A good leader applies a coherent vision of their company and takes it all the way down to the granular level so that each person on their team is being utilized to the full extent of their talents. It sounds like a no-brainer, but very often, I find that companies are sitting on hidden treasures (in the form of their employees), because someone somewhere made the decision that this person belongs in one place, when in fact their talents are much better suited to a different department. So the vision was and has remained a core tenet of my leadership style.

The second component of my leadership style is rooted in democracy. This is personal to me; others may prefer a top-down approach to leadership—a militaristic command style if you will. However, for me, this is just not as effective. By encouraging my team members to arm themselves with autonomy and become more active participants in company decisions and directions, I empower them to tap into their own leadership potential. I have found this democratic approach to team building has allowed my employees to feel seen and heard as individuals, and it has therefore created a stronger bond between us as a result. I would caution any business professional, entrepreneur, or leader not to underestimate the power of validating your team members. Loyalty is a precious commodity that no amount of money can purchase.

Learning Leadership without a Mentor

Over the years, the efficacy of mentorship has only become more and more of a prerequisite to great leadership. But that begs the question: what should those of us who don't have a mentor to learn from directly do? Are we hopelessly disadvantaged? Not necessarily. Throughout my career, I have never actually had a mentor or coach, but that also didn't get in the way of consuming everything I could from the resources I had at my disposal. In our digital age, it's never been easier to learn the secrets to successful leadership. My recommendation is this: If you don't have a mentor, be proactive in your independent learning! In short, study not only the successes of other professionals you admire but also their mistakes.

Elon Musk, Mark Zuckerberg, Jeff Bezos, even Oprah... The beauty of the internet is that many of the personal details of the giants of industry that have come before us are now just a Google search away. I don't limit myself to simply business professionals either. When it comes to mentors, I generally admire anyone who has the tenacity to see their goals through. However, while I would never discredit the value of face-to-face mentorship, I also do not believe it's the only way to become an effective leader.

As I was planning to develop my company, I spent a great deal of time studying the habits and leadership characteristics of the individuals I admired. However, it was more than just a cursory search. If you want to truly understand what makes someone effective in their position, treat your research as if you're building a case study! Write out the timeline of the leader in question, or the company you're researching. What were their initial setbacks? How did they overcome them, and what might you have done differently? Do the decisions they make resonate with your own leadership style, or would you have approached the situation with a different mentality? Write all of it down! The more you write, the more you will understand about yourself.

It is only the leaders who are fully aware of their own *limitations*, as well as their inherent *talents*, that are able to be effective in directing others!

Leadership in Action

Dr. Aby Lillian Mamboleo

Dr. Aby Lillian Mamboleo has come a long way since her native Nairobi, Kenya. She is an accomplished CEO, entrepreneur, and a role model living her motto-driven course, "I'm a B.I.T."(Billionaire in Training). She is the founder of the publishing imprint, Mamboleo Media Group. Aby co-authored Business, Life & the Universe, Volume 6, *which is a No. 1 Amazon bestseller.*[2] *Additionally, she co-authored the entrepreneurial book,* The Entrepreneur's Funding Guide: 100 Places to Get Over $100K to Fund Your Business.[3]

Achieving her success through service and heart, Dr. Mamboleo is a recognized consultant and thought leader. Having honed her skills as an advisor in the staffing industry, she went on to teach business owners innovative ways to manage, grow, and scale their business.

A Powerful Vision, a Powerful Dream

Growing up, I spent a great deal of time with my dad, as my mom was pregnant with my younger siblings, seemingly back-to-back. As a result, my dad's auspicious dreams about becoming a successful lawyer were imprinted on me at a young age. I couldn't have

---

2 Corey Poirier, BLU Talks Presents: Business, Life and the Universe, vol. 6 (Ottawa, Ontario: Canadian ISBN, 2022).

3 Constance Moonzwe and Aby L. Mamboleo, The Entrepreneurs Funding Guide: 100 Places to Get Over $100k to Fund Your Business (Scotts Valley, CA: CreateSpace Independent Publishing Platform, 2017).

told you exactly what it was that a lawyer did back then, but I knew with every fiber of my being that that's what I was going to be. I was so sure of it, in fact, that I would audaciously introduce myself to any new person I met as, "Aby Mamboleo, lawyer." I couldn't have known it then, but this self-projection was really just the art of putting a vision into practice, making it real by already believing you've taken on that role. In my mind's eye, it was already a done deal.

While this mindset may have initially come across as a game to others, it wasn't without merit: I did achieve my childhood dream and graduated sometime later with a JD/MBA. Initially, my undergraduate degree was in communication studies. I figured I must learn how to communicate, negotiate, and handle myself as an expert professional if I was ever going to make it into law school. While I was able to play this vision out for real in my professional career, I found my truest and greatest success as an entrepreneur. Today, I mainly use my law degree to help prepare, read, and negotiate contracts. I have also periodically taught "Introduction to Law" to a group of aspiring paralegals at a community college.

Ultimately, my career aspirations have changed some since that crystal vision I enacted throughout most of my childhood. Yet I can say with some certainty that I would not have become who I am today had it not been for that deliberate practice of mentally placing myself into the future, and feeling the weight of my own personal success story (even if it had not yet come).

Becoming a B.I.T.

I started my first business before I was even legally able to do so—I wasn't even yet eighteen. Yes, I started my very first business while I was still in high school—and in Kenya, mind you. The business itself was simple in concept: I would make little bracelets and other charms and sell them to students like myself or else to anyone interested. From the onset, I was thrust into (or rather created) a leadership role. My siblings were both my team and my first "employees," and I was not shy about putting them to work. Still, looking back, I think that's where my leadership journey really began. I've always been entrepreneurial in spirit, but it was that venture that solidified the idea inside of me forever.

Picture this if you can: a young, precocious teenager in Kenya telling anyone and everyone who will listen, "I'm going to be a lawyer, but right now, I'm just a millionaire in training." Oh yes, I had star-studded dreams even back then. Interestingly enough, the mental discipline I had instilled in myself in crafting and sustaining such a detailed vision of my future as a lawyer paid dividends in other areas of my life as well. I did eventually reach those precious millions just like I'd forecasted! Afterwards, I realized that I needed a new goal, a new challenge to sink my teeth into. So I have since revised my introduction: I am now a B.I.T.—a Billionaire in Training.

Born into Leadership: What Defines a Great Leader?

I like to say that as the eldest of all of my siblings, I was born into a leadership position. It was my job to set the example for my brothers and sisters to follow, and as a result, I acquired various leadership components by sheer osmosis along the way.

However, being born into leadership doesn't necessarily make you an effective leader right off the bat. Somewhat ironically, one of my greatest struggles as a leader, particularly in a professional capacity, has been that I am simply not a micromanager. Not only does it not come naturally to me, but for a long time, I really did not know how to do it! While most people would consider this a good thing by itself, my professional experience has taught me that there are people who actively prefer—sometimes even need—to be micromanaged in order to thrive. But hand-holding has never been my area of expertise. In fact, my leadership style has always been more of the laissez-faire variety: you do what's needed to get the job done, and I'll do what I need to do to make sure things proceed on schedule.

While some people can excel in this kind of autonomous environment, there are others who quickly start to feel adrift, uncared for, undervalued, etc. Thus, one of the major lessons I've had to learn as I continue to pivot, evolve, and grow my leadership style is that whoever you think you are as a leader cannot be a static, unchanging idea. A great leader, in my opinion, is not defined by the type of leadership he or she employs in the workplace, but rather by how well that person can read and adapt to the needs of their team in order to achieve a unified goal. After all, you can't change the personalities of your entire team, can you?

Overcoming my natural inclination to keep a certain distance as a leader was not easy. However, with time, I learned how to provide clear and direct feedback to team members who did need some degree of hand-holding or regular approval. Furthermore, I went so far as to create checklists to guide me when dealing with such situations. What I've found to be true is that more often than not, people who desire this type of helicopter supervision lack confidence in themselves and conviction in their abilities. Thus, one of the ways my leadership has changed over the years is that I now take an active approach in building the professional self-esteem of these employees by empowering them to take on greater and greater responsibilities, so they can get the feedback they desire not just from me but from their peers as well.

When I think about my leadership role today, I like to think that I serve as something akin to the Chief Encouraging Officer. My job is to support my team and help them achieve their goals; I am as much a mentor as the person in charge. Viewing myself as a mentor, rather than strictly a boss, has made it easier for me to give my employees the help they need, while also maintaining the space to allow them to carve out their own independence.

The Challenge of Motivating a Gen-Z Workforce

Culturally, there are no two ways about it: a workforce comprised of ever-increasing numbers of Gen-Z employees feels, acts, and thinks differently than their predecessors. It follows, then, that when it comes to motivating my current team, the processes and procedures are markedly different from the teams I have worked with in the past.

While critics are often quick to slap this demographic with a reputation for entitlement, or a lack of work ethic, what I've found is that Gen-Zers are simply motivated by a different set of values and reward standards. In the past, the dynamic was very different, and I was able to motivate my team by concentrating on their desires for fitness and better health. As a company, we would run half marathons together, or I would offer to pay for the gym memberships of my employees because that's what was important to them outside of the workplace. However, today I would argue that the primary motivations among young people are money and work-life balance.

Commenting on the latter, I've come to think of this not so much as having a fully-remote position, having a ping-pong table in the office, or a vending machine that makes gluten-free smoothies, but rather, I believe that the generation of today is concerned with feeling connected to the place and people they work with. Thus, I've made it a mission of mine to drastically increase the amount of teamwork projects and out-of-office activities we engage in. This not only helps strengthen the bonds between co-workers, but I believe it also serves to solidify the point that we care about one another in our company culture. This is not a 9-to-5 lifetime sentence; I want people to take pride and satisfaction in the work they do.

The second component of motivating a team of Gen-Zers is, of course, money. This is hands down the biggest motivator of young people today. Truthfully, I can understand their position. We live in difficult times right now, and the future can often seem daunting and uncertain. To mitigate some of these fears and keep morale high, I frequently offer bonuses or opportunities for my employees to capture more money if they are able to prove themselves or demonstrate further value. This circles back around to being a "Chief Encouraging Officer." Sometimes it is just as valuable to my team to be encouraged in achieving their financial goals as it is to actually offer a salary increase or a bonus. In individual meetings, I will often ask an employee about their long-term goals. If someone mentions that they want to make six figures, for example, in the next two to three years, I will sit down with them and help draw out a plan to make that a reality. In this way, I strive to motivate my team, not just by offering lucrative handouts, but by also encouraging them to construct a vision with an accompanying plan.

Once my employees realize that I am genuinely and earnestly invested in their success, it becomes that much easier to motivate them to tackle whatever challenges we might face.

Advice to the Burgeoning Entrepreneur/ Leader

Looking back on my own journey through college and law school and the subsequent enterprises that I've established since then, I would not change much about my own journey. There were hard lessons that I needed to learn along the way, but ultimately, they shaped and molded me into the person I am now. However, if I had the opportunity to relate some of the most impactful lessons I've learned about quality leadership, here is what I would offer the entrepreneur who's just finding their footing.

Effective listening is a skill worth its weight in gold. Ironically, listening is one of the leadership responsibilities, which does not appear in the job description. A good listener can see the world through the eyes of others and is instrumental in helping us understand different cultural perspectives as well as the larger, macro picture. Becoming an effective listener is a key tenet in leading people with different personalities towards a mutual goal. As a leader, you want to let your coworkers know that they are appreciated, valued, and loved—doing that plays a key role in helping them reach their maximum potential. Listening—true listening—leads to personal growth and allows an individual to remain open-minded.

Manage your people and resources well—delegate. Delegation is one of those buzzwords that often gets tossed around so much that it has begun to lose some of its meaning. Delegating is easy, but delegating well is not; it's an acquired skill. True delegation isn't simply about handing things off that you don't want to deal with yourself. As a leader, delegation is about selecting appropriate opportunities to empower your team members to complete the task at hand. If you only delegate the undesirable or impossible tasks to your team, their perception of you will be of the lazy leader, and they will take their behavioral cues from you in this regard. Instead, be thoughtful and intentional when you decide to disperse the workload.

Invest in yourself. Education should not stop with a university degree. The greatest business leaders and entrepreneurs around the world take an active and unyielding interest in learning. Fundamentally, they understand that there is always something new to learn, a new skill to acquire, or a new, more effective approach to problem-solving. As you grow into your own leadership style, continually reinvest in your skills. Take courses, join masterminds, and network with other professionals. You will never be so successful that you can no longer benefit from learning.

Don't Wait for Permission to Lead

Megan Hightower Martins

Megan Hightower Martins, SHRM-SCP, GPHR is the Founder and CEO of POPS Enabled and serves as a subject matter expert and exam developer for the HR Certification Institute.

Megan has extensive experience helping companies win employer choice awards year after year through fostering globally inclusive and engaging initiatives. She's spent more than a decade optimizing and automating digital solutions for SMBs, start-ups, and high-growth, mission-driven, globally dispersed remote workplaces.

Having supported operations throughout EMEA, APAC, and LATAM, her expertise includes global expansion, compliance, leading international investigations, systems design, remote collaboration and culture design, and process optimization in complex corporate structures.

As a strategist and trusted consultant, she helps other businesses architect world-class employee experiences, advance corporate strategy, and access global talent—all in a cost-effective manner.

Lessons on Leadership from My Daughter

There are a lot of different ways to look at leadership qualities, and probably even more methods of measuring these qualities. My daughter, for instance, may be described by some as "bossy" or a tad "too vocal." I choose to echo Cheryl Sandberg's perspective that she's simply exhibiting "executive leadership skills." My mom told me that just the other day that she was at the neighborhood pool with her brother and five other neighborhood boys. Despite being the youngest of the bunch, she was undisputedly orchestrating the show, directing everyone where to go and how to play the games. I recognize that as leadership qualities. In truth, she's braver than I am in that way. Yes, she's got some honing in to do, but I would never want to stifle her, or anyone else's, unique and natural leadership abilities. It takes tremendous confidence and a lot of time—especially as a woman—before many of us can step into a meeting and address a room full of seasoned (and predominantly male) executives with poise, grace, and authority.

Frankly, these are the types of women I admire the most (the ones like my daughter). I turn into a sponge in their presence, trying to soak up everything from their mannerisms to their speaking style and abilities. However, truth be told, my own leadership characteristics are quite different, and they were definitely something I had to learn over time rather than something that I inherited genetically.

Early Lessons on Motivation

When it comes to personality tests, I'm what you might call a golden retriever. I generally get along with everyone, could sit with anyone in the lunchroom, and I always made a point to avoid the unnecessary drama that tends to be analogous with adolescence. I was predisposed towards perfectionism in everything I set my mind to do—whether it was sports, academics, or work—which at the time was both a blessing and a curse. My determination afforded me the opportunity to compete in national championships, receive "all-district" and "all-conference" accolades, landed me on the national honor roll, and even secured me a real job by the age of fifteen.

My first exposure to "leadership" was when I became a shift supervisor at Wendy's during my junior year of high school. It definitely wasn't a glamorous job, but it did teach me a great deal about team dynamics, motivation, hard work, and commitment. I would regularly work until two or three in the morning, unloading deliveries, counting down drawers, and closing the books before arriving home to complete any last-minute homework I'd procrastinated on completing. I was always the last person to leave and didn't stay in the office to duck out on the unpleasant tasks, like scrubbing the hoods, washing dishes, and cleaning out drains. I intentionally stayed on the floor to help the crew clean so they could leave at a decent hour.

Thus, rather than any formal style of leadership, I would say that my modus operandi has always been simply to focus on my own work ethic, acting always out of my own moral code, and treating those around me with dignity and respect. As a waitress or bartender, I certainly didn't have any formal authority, but I noticed early on that by going out of my way to be helpful by taking on responsibilities outside of my own, it became contagious. While I've never done any of this with the deliberate intent to "get something in return" even to this day, this model has never really failed. If you just keep your eyes open, I've found that you can learn a lot about leadership in the most unlikely of places.

Here are some other tips about motivation and engagement that don't cost your company a dime and build significant value:

- Offer exposure to various specialties and areas of the business, and provide them exposure to both lead and build rapport with other key leaders in the organization.
- Find out what aspects of your colleague's jobs they really excel at and enjoy and which ones they might find less appealing. I'll say it again, again, and again: the gesture of genuinely showing you give a damn about others' professional growth and overall employee experience will come back to you tenfold. I've witnessed this not only in my personal experience and in that of others who practice similar values, but conversely, I've also seen ineffective and often detrimental outcomes for leaders who fail to acknowledge and value their teams.
- Automate, integrate, and build efficiencies. I've seen a lot of wins in the area of automation and systems designs because it can be incredibly impactful on the internal mood of a company when you put the right systems, tools, and automation in place to free people's time so they can focus on more challenging aspects of their work. Moving away from the transactional and guiding team members towards the transformational goes a long way in validating their worth, leveraging their capabilities, and advancing their careers.
- Be accessible, supportive, open to criticism, and acknowledge when you screw up. In other words, behave like a respectable, accountable, approachable human being who operates with empathy rather than judgment. I'm not sure about you, but I certainly can't do my best work when I feel like

someone is constantly looking over my shoulder with criticism. The trending theme here is psychological safety. For me, this all starts by giving those around me the same amount of grace and kindness that I would appreciate from my peers and leaders.
- Prioritize diversity, equity, and inclusion. Belonging is critical in building a successful business and a winning culture. Businesses that successfully maintain diverse representation across the organization, particularly in leadership and executive roles, convey the message that everyone has an opportunity to succeed.

Know Your People

All the years—far more than I'd care to admit—that I spent in the service industry working my way through school culminated in the skills and drive I would need to be successful as an individual and as a leader. I quickly observed that authority in title is insignificant without one's ability to build strong relationships built on a foundation of trust and respect.

For example, all too often businesses promote their "rock star" individual contributors to management under the misguided belief it's the only way to retain their top performers. The assumption is that they'll freely pass on their wealth of knowledge to enable that same greatness in their direct reports, thus magically creating more rock stars. Often they're shocked to witness a sudden deterioration of that department's productivity, achievements, and morale. Your MVP has been reassigned to spend their day running meetings, setting KPIs, scheduling one-on-ones, managing time off requests, reviewing others' (likely less star-studded than their own) performance, and handling interpersonal issues—typically without an ounce of managerial training. Only then, at the detriment of your former MVP's self-confidence and after deflating the spirit of the entire team, do we learn that management was not the right fit.

On the extreme end, I've seen these individuals compete against their own direct reports, undermine or take credit for others' work, and received complaints from their subordinates that led to investigations, and even terminations. Everyone suffers and disengagement ensues.

I encourage organizations to be very intentional about how they recognize achievement and subsequently position people for success. Before blindly offering promotions to a role in which the individual has yet to display aptitude or interest, make sure you understand what gets them out of bed in the morning. Offer a dual path for promotion in your organization, one that ensures competent managers lead teams, and that allows key contributors to have a distinguished path for advancement in both title and compensation.

Speak Up

While there was no singular epiphany, or "aha" moment, in my career, one of the biggest challenges that I encountered came being thrust into a leadership role quickly, and unexpectedly.

I first became acutely aware of this dilemma when working with some incredibly competent Ivy League graduate executives. In my awe and abundant respect for these people, I made the assumption that they "just had it." There was no way that I could offer any insights that they weren't already aware of. I would assume that it was me who was missing something. "They've already thought through that—it's not even my area of expertise," I would say to myself. Turns out they hadn't.

By not trusting my own voice, I was withholding what I knew to be valuable information, which wasn't helpful for the team or myself. I learned quickly that if I didn't say something, it was unlikely that anyone else would either. I realized that I had to be vocal. The way that you treat yourself, particularly in moments of doubt, is the way you condition others to treat you as well.

That said, we all have insecurities and experience uncertainty from time to time. I recently heard an incredible icon who speaks in front of an audience as huge as tens of thousands of people say that they still get physically sick before walking on stage. I can't tell you how refreshing it has been to see that kind of raw vulnerability from our powerhouse leaders. I applaud and appreciate those who are bravely and boldly vulnerable. It not only humanizes them as leaders but also inspires the rest of us that we're all capable of overcoming whatever flaws or quirks we may have been blessed with.

Allow yourself to briefly acknowledge whatever self-doubt may exist, smile humorously, and forge ahead in spite of it.

Integrity Is Everything

On more than one occasion now, I've found myself at the crux of what's ethically the right thing to do being grossly at odds with activities in which executives have attempted to coerce me into taking part.

I don't share even this vague nugget of information lightly. In fact, my initial draft for this book ducked the topic of integrity and corporate ethics entirely. But in the spirit of authenticity, any reflections about what's shaped my understanding of leadership would have lacked substance had I glossed over the monumental role of ethics and integrity when discussing leadership.

My experiences have made it painstakingly clear that living and breathing integrity is a nonnegotiable, baseline requirement for anyone who wants to be a true leader. You don't have to look far in history, society, or current events to understand that irreversible and catastrophic impacts occur when people in power resort to lying, cheating, and stealing. The same effects consistently play out in the corporate world when there's disregard for potential adverse effects of their actions on people's financial, emotional, or physical well-being. I've yet to witness the latter produce lasting, or even temporary, success for those who engage in dishonest behavior.

Despite the rare and unpleasant run-ins with leadership gone wrong, I wholeheartedly believe that such individuals are the minority. For the large majority of us who show up with the fullest intent to get it right, we will undoubtedly make mistakes. Sometimes big mistakes. Yet, even then, the only real failure is shying away from taking proper accountability and ignoring the teachable moment. I've found that people are met with a great deal more understanding and forgiveness when we don't let our ego stand in the way.

Advice for a Younger Me

If I had to do everything all over again, or if I was to offer some wisdom that I've learned along the way to someone just starting their leadership journey, here's what I would say:

Be you. Be kind. It's tempting whenever you start a new role or get promoted to say to yourself, "I have to prove to everyone that I deserve to be here." In actuality, that belief is rooted in insecurity, in a scarcity mindset. The winning formula for success has always been to show up with kindness, dedication, and an open mind. The only thing you have to prove is that you're worthy of the team's trust and support.

We rise by lifting others. Regardless of what position you hold, each and every one of us has the responsibility to elevate ourselves and those around us. For those of us fortunate enough to be in a leadership role, we bear this responsibility even more heavily.

You can't fake good culture. The values you embody, the ways in which you treat others, and the relationships you build across every function of your organization will make or break your ability to lead effectively. Before you concern yourself with a company's external brand or reputation, it's imperative to understand that it all begins with internal culture. How can you live the values that you preach? How can you cement them within your organization, from the C-suite executives down to the recently hired intern?

You don't need a formal title to lead. If you're waiting for the green light, the official stamp of approval or some other abstract, universal nod to start acting like a leader, you might find yourself waiting a long time. Being a leader never has to be more complicated than setting quality standards and doing what we can to improve the environment in which we all want to work, play, and live.

Without a foundation of trust, respect, and integrity, you're dead on arrival. If leaders don't embody the company's core values or consistently reward individuals who behave unethically, all other attempts to improve the workplace are futile and quickly overshadowed.

Greatness in leadership is built on the basic foundation of respect, authenticity, trust, and compassion. In other words, it's really not that hard; everything we needed to know about leadership, we already learned in kindergarten.

PART TWO:

TEAMING

Lessons that demonstrate together is better

Resource*full* Leadership

Brett Currier

Brett Currier is the Founder and CEO of VetGigs, a talent marketplace with the mission to help veterans and military spouses find a new purpose after the military through lucrative careers in technology, consulting, and other professional services. Veterans build a wealth of skills and experience in the military. VetGigs aims to give them the best opportunities possible to carry that value into the civilian workforce.

Brett started his career in the US Army and Army National Guard, where he served for twelve years. His service included a tour in Operation Iraqi Freedom and Operation New Dawn. Brett has had the unfortunate experience of losing several "battle buddies" to suicide. He now seeks to make a scalable impact on the 22+ veterans a day who lose their battle tragically. Brett is an alumnus of Deloitte Consulting, where he was a key part in the launch of the Higher Education Future of Work and Future of Commercial Talent Acquisition service offerings. He now works at Huron Consulting Group, where they have shown incredible support of the VetGigs' mission.

To learn more about how the VetGigs team is helping the veteran community and business leaders with the war on talent, visit www.vetgigs.com. *Veterans begin their journey to finding new purpose after the military through VetGigs, where business leaders can access world-class veteran talent for their organizations.*

The Great Resignation

We are currently in one of the most turbulent and competitive periods on record regarding talent. Some call it the "Great Resignation," while others, "a new chapter in the war on talent." Deb Tenenbaum is a Board Member of VetGigs and the Chief Human Resource Officer of AppDirect. She recently told me, "There has been a self-awakening of talent in corporate America during COVID, as knowledge workers have been isolated. They find themselves wondering, 'Do I really want to be doing what I'm doing? I can work from anywhere.'" This is an observation I see echoed by executives across commercial talent acquisition through my work in consulting.

So What Do We Do About It?

Gallup Research shows the number one reason employees leave is a lack of career opportunities at their organization. This is driven by the second highest reason: the relationship with their manager. Business units experiencing poor retention often have managers purely focused on tasks instead of how their people can grow to their highest potential. Higher performing business units are often run by leaders who invest in their team's *individual* professional development areas of growth and not just the areas that would immediately benefit the organization. In other words, keep the focus on individual needs.

Both in the army and at Deloitte Consulting, I served under leaders who used this approach. It resulted in making me a more well-rounded and operationally capable professional, and it also kept me working at the organization longer than would have been optimal were I only considering financial incentives. This professional development investment does not need to be in terms of building expensive programs, paying for costly training programs or certifications. They can be as simple as making space in your team's day to develop themselves outside their regular tasks. Examples include leading lunch and learns, shadowing a leader who is an experienced mentor, joining a company mentorship program, or getting involved in a cross functional project.

As leaders, most of us are bound by resource limitations, and we would like to put excess funds into raises, bonus pools, and shareholder returns when possible. I approach the issue by following the process described below, to seek out resources beyond my organization.

Understand the Needs of My Team

Each employee owns their career development, but resourceful leaders facilitate and guide that growth like a coach bringing out the best performance in their players. This is best accomplished by providing the space for growth and a detailed plan for it. The plan helps ensure that resources—like talent's time and money—aren't wasted by participating in programs or activities that aren't beneficial in accomplishing the team member's goals. Understanding the needs, goals, and career aspirations of my team is an ongoing task. The ongoing nature is helpful because they know it is a priority for me, and it is alright for them to shift their goals either as they meet their objectives or progress in their career. Together we chart development plans, discuss measurable performance indicators, and talk about the resources available to get them there. Sometimes these are resources I provide, but often they are what is available through the person's "nets."

Everyone Has a Resource Net

We each belong to communities such as geographic, ethnic, religious/spiritual, alumni, and/or many other potential affiliations. Many resources are available to support our communities, such as mentorship, training, certification, job placement, and other professional development tools. Each resource has a narrow scope of value, like an individual piece of rope in a net, so it is up to us to determine how these ropes can weave together to generate the holistic support we need. You can look at resources in five main buckets: networking, on-the-job learning, on-the-job teaching, self-improvement, and social impact.

You Don't Have to Be the Net, You Only Need to Be a Knot

As leaders, we can provide on-the-job learning and teaching, but we often don't have the resources to provide that holistic value entirely within our organization for all our team's networking, self-improvement, and social impact needs. We can help our talent discover resources available to them that can be used to accomplish their professional development goals. I first discovered this technique as a noncommissioned officer (NCO) in the US Army. We were often tasked with accomplishing difficult objects and given less-than-ideal resources to make it happen. I often would have soldiers with excellent potential, but I couldn't get them into all the training that would be ideal to develop them to their potential. I saw some of the best leaders I served with go above and beyond to reach out to other government agencies to see how we could cross-train with them at no cost and get creative with the free educational resources we could find online. For years, we had one of the most highly trained military police companies in the US because of that strategy and won several unit citations that recognized our heightened readiness. These leaders knew that they couldn't provide all the ropes in the net needed to support their people, so they became the knot that tied all the relevant resources together.

I began using this analogy for the Veteran Community, but I now use it to mentor civilian talent as well. I ask questions about the person's background to better understand where they can look for resources. The person's answers to my questions allow me to adapt the net analogy to what makes sense for them.

My Development Discussions with My Team

I spend a lot of time having development discussions with fellow veterans, my team at VetGigs, my peers in consulting, and those reporting to me on my projects as a management consultant. It starts with learning about them. I ask these questions:

- What are your long-term goals?
- What professional groups are you a part of?
- What community groups are you a part of?
- What geographic areas are you tied to (hometown, where you live now, where you work, etc.)?

- What do you consider a core part of your identity (ethnic background, gender, religious beliefs, etc.)?

I ask about their goals to help determine the destination they are trying to get to. I ask about the groups they identify with because that helps me determine what communities they are a part of. Those communities may have resources to help them on their way. If the person is a member of a professional organization, we can investigate the potential of free training that may be helpful in their development plan. The cities they live and work in may have their own development programs, ranging from free training to mentorship programs. It is common for religious and ethnic groups to have their own mentorship and training programs, examples being, the Sikh Mentorship Program (SMP) or the Black in Corporate Virtual Mentorship program. Many community resources can offer tremendous support. We need to simply invest the time to get to know our people, identify which groups they are a part of, and help them to use those resources to meet their goals. I have always been able to find resources needed to facilitate my mentee's development plan by combining what my organizations could provide with those available to my mentee as a member of their communities.

Build a Value Network

With VetGigs, I have built a network of organizations to provide value to the veteran community because we each have unique ways of serving the community. I identified career life cycles where different needs arose. Some veterans may need a laptop, which we can get them, along with training on how to use it, through one of our partners,

Tech For Troops. Other veterans may require training to qualify for higher-paying technology, start-up, and consulting jobs. In that case, we steer them into programs where they can get free certifications from top universities that demonstrate their industry knowledge and directly qualify them for positions. Some veterans need specific mental health resources, and VetGigs has partners who offer psychotherapy of various forms. When our veterans who have used these programs find work on VetGigs, we donate a portion of any profits on the platform back to the organizations that helped them, to reinvest in their missions. Together we provide exponentially more value to our communities than any of us could on our own. This value accelerator demonstrates the power of the resource net every day, as veterans and military spouses move through our programs to address their needs.

Spotting Opportunities for Mutual Value and Investing in Your Partners

The organizations involved in this process benefit from taking part, in addition to the participants who it is intended to support. It works because everyone involved gets something back. Let's review VetGigs's partnership flow as an example:

We at VetGigs connect a veteran without a computer to Tech For Troops, which offers free laptops and training to the veteran community. Next, they come back to VetGigs to receive a professional development plan mapping out how to achieve their goals and to create a VetGigs account where they can get matched with employment opportunities. VetGigs sends users to our partners who provide a free Coursera license that can be used to attain the certifications necessary to meet their career goals. When the veteran or military spouse finds work on VetGigs, we donate a percentage of any profit generated back to the organizations the user participated in, so we can reinvest in the mission. We are all able to provide exponentially more value because we work together. Without the program participants, the resources for participants would cease to operate. VetGigs offers our partner organizations a new way to generate revenue beyond grants or donations in a way that supports veterans and military spouses. These partnership programs enable VetGigs to reach our target market without incurring the difficulty of marketing to individuals.

Resourceful leadership requires looking for these opportunities to put value chains together, both for your team and the groups taking part. Participants in a program provide the benefit of showing higher resources, which allows them to maintain—and even grow—funding. I always look beyond that, though, and have helped our partners through monetary donations and by providing employment services to groups focusing on training. Organizations with a training focus are often evaluated by their ability to show their program participants get great jobs, so partnerships with employment service groups are mutually beneficial.

The value your team provides for the groups taking part may simply be having more participants in the groups they target. Other ways may include employment opportunities, donations of money or equipment, services, or providing visibility for their organization. Demonstrating the process and where everyone provides and receives their usefulness will enable a fast setup of partnerships.

In Summary

Resourceful leadership is vital in order to compete in this new stage of the war on talent. Investing the time to build professional development plans grows a positive relationship between managers and their team in addition to making staff feel assured that they have growth opportunities at the organization. The resources required to support teams do not have to come from your organization alone, but can be sourced from the communities that your mentees are a member of. Building a network of organizations to provide support can seem like a daunting task; however, it can come quite naturally when we look at it as a chain of value based on what each group needs, and seeing where each group can contribute based on their areas of focus. Resource*full* leaders know that to win the war on talent, you need to invest in your people. Follow these methods and you will go a long way towards establishing your organization as the epitome of an attractive workplace.

Leading from the Front

Lance Graulich

Lance Graulich hosts the top 50 business podcast "Eye on Franchising." He founded and serves as CEO of ION Franchising, an industry-leading franchise consulting and development group that represents over 750 franchise brands and business opportunities in every imaginable category. Lance helps prospective entrepreneurs find their perfect franchise for free. He also assists independent business owners in creating a franchise system.

Lance started out in the family business on Wall Street after receiving an economics degree. He then joined a TGI Fridays franchise in Phoenix as a key executive and was vital to the rapid growth of this $225-million organization. Mr Graulich was a multiunit, multistate franchisee of Wingstop and Krispy Kreme Doughnuts.

He has created countless start-up brands. He is the founder of a donut chain called Pinkbox in Las Vegas. His latest start-up bakery project is with a Food Network star.

As a business start-up expert with more than twenty-five years of experience, he has served as president of various franchise advisory councils and boards advising emerging franchise brands. He has helped a multitude of companies grow efficiently and effectively. Lance routinely provides advisory services to private equity firms covering the restaurant industry as well.

Raised on Leadership

You might say I was raised to be a leader. Both my grandfathers were entrepreneurs, and my dad was a partner in a big Wall Street firm. I always tell people there are three major pillars to building wealth: one is real estate, one is owning your own business, and the other piece is Wall Street—stocks, bonds, and investments. One of my grandpas was a real estate attorney who bought buildings. My other grandfather was a Polish immigrant that nobody could ever understand who successfully built a chain of supermarkets and enjoyed driving his big fat Cadillac and smoking a big cigar. With my dad on Wall Street, I call it the trifecta: I got to experience all three investment pillars play out right in front of me at a young age.

To top it off, my mom was a school principal. So I had strong leadership exhibited all around while growing up in New York. Where I lived back then, kids would go away to camp to do activities like swimming, sailing, waterskiing, and other sports. As I got older, I won awards for leadership. At a young age, what you start to learn about leadership is that people want to follow you because you have the answers. And at a young age, I started realizing that I had the answers, and more importantly, I wanted to find out the answers and I had the vision to do so.

I was always what a friend of mine called "the rainmaker." I felt very comfortable being the leader and getting everybody pumped up. I was always that rainmaker who felt comfortable putting myself out there, going forward, and clearing the path. When I got into team sports, it was the same type of thing.

A Future in Franchising

I thought I was going to work on Wall Street and be a stockbroker like my dad until, eventually, I realized it was kind of boring. I didn't feel a certain energy that I felt like I should. We had a very close friend of the family we called Uncle Steve, although he wasn't really an uncle. He knew I was bored, and he wanted to build a TGI Fridays franchise, so that became the first opportunity I had to get into franchising. I moved from New York to Arizona, and I became what was called a "manager in development." I eventually made my way up to regional manager with TGI Fridays in a five-year timeframe.

Leaving the state was a big pivot for me. I had the best upbringing and the most supportive parents. My parents never missed an event that I was in, but I thought I needed to find my own path. So when Uncle Steven presented the option to go to Arizona and help him grow the four TGI Fridays restaurant franchises he had just bought, I took him up on it. Five years later, there were over sixty-five restaurants doing over $225 million a year. He mentored me, and I helped him grow that business. I really got to participate in the growth process to understand how to grow a big business quickly.

Now I'm one of the largest franchise brokers in the US. I represent over seven hundred franchise brands in every category. I've also owned quite a few franchises and created my own restaurant concepts. I've found that many people are interested in creating that one opportunity that takes them out of the corporate grind so they can really control their own destinies and build financial freedom.

Self-Awareness and Becoming a Leader

My greatest struggle, one that was very pivotal for me, was learning self-awareness and how important it is when it comes to leadership. Two of my role models, my father and grandfather, were very tough leaders. From seeing that my whole life, I thought leadership was all about being that strong.

So there I was, a former New Yorker with that New York attitude, hitting Arizona and running a shift in a restaurant where I was a new assistant manager, and I wasn't getting the results that I expected. People weren't receptive to my leadership style—mainly because I wasn't self-aware enough. A veteran waitress, Karen, who was a shift leader, said to me, "Do you mind if I give you some feedback?" I said, "Please do." She gave me feedback that I was an ass, and that I didn't treat people appropriately. I was too tough. I didn't request. I demanded too much.

After that, I started studying leadership and realized I needed to establish rapport with people instead of just barking commands at them. I needed to lead by example. I needed to be out front showing them how things get done and participate as opposed to sitting in my ivory tower, cracking the whip.

It was definitely a key moment in my early career. The way I looked at it was I didn't think I was a moldable piece of clay. But really, I was a baby in leadership, and that's exactly what I was: a moldable piece of clay. Thankfully, I was young enough to be able to adapt. The older we get, the more stuck in our ways we tend to get. I listened to Karen, took it to heart, and continued to ask for her advice. I made what you could call a 180-degree shift due to Karen's tutelage and my own studying to become more self-aware.

What did I study? I read leadership books. *The One Minute Manager* by Ken Blanchard was a big book in those days.[4] I learned there's a difference between management

---

[4] Kenneth H. Blanchard and Spencer Johnson, The One Minute Manager: The Quickest Way to Increase Your Own Prosperity (New York City, NY: HarperCollins, 1994).

and leadership. I learned that it all comes back to "There's no I in a team." I went from being this autocratic, demanding person to truly leading by example and really becoming more of a servant leader.

In the restaurant business, you have peaks and valleys in business levels. It can be really stressful for the staff, and the leader's job is to coordinate what's going on. For the same reason, a captain of a ship in rough seas is not below deck. They're up front steering because there are a lot of paths you can take. So in the middle of a busy shift, I would always be present and visible, and the staff would feel reassured that I was around.

As I shifted gears, within a couple of months, the staff all got to see what a team player I was, and soon I was their favorite manager to work with. At the end of the day, leadership is not about being liked; it's about being respected. People wouldn't call out on their shift for me because they would feel like they were letting me and the team down. With great leadership, you're more likely to have low turnover and callout rates.

Motivation via Education

There are a lot of ways to motivate people. As I've matured as a leader, I focus on motivating by example and by educating. When people come to me looking for businesses, they're future entrepreneurs—I call them "future-preneurs." They're not quite entrepreneurs yet, but they want to own their own businesss. When they first meet me, sometimes they're pretty soft-spoken and unsure of themselves. They don't have a high level of confidence that they'll ever be able to be their own boss.

I start with, "Let's talk about your 'what.'" And they say, "You mean your 'why?'" I tell them, "Everybody has around the same 'why.' We all want to do some sort of good. We all want to help our family. We all want some sort of financial freedom. We all want to set our own schedule and not be beholden to a boss. That's a lot of people's 'why.' The 'what' is 'What is your investment level? What can you invest in a franchise based on your personal financials? Is it $10,000? Is it $100,000?'" I tell them financing is available. Then I ask them, "What kind of role do you want to play in your future business?"

I talk about what they want: "Do you want to work full time in this business? Or do you want to be a semi-absentee owner, where you stay at your day job for a period of time, and then you gradually move over to an owner-operator model?" So they start to get really motivated and inspired that they can do this. What I do to motivate people is to educate them by providing information on business start-ups and finding their perfect business based on their what.

As a franchise consultant, I am also a franchise coach, consultant, and strategist. I help clients see their future in franchising. Leadership is all about making people see what can be. You are the visionary, and people follow your vision—the one you create based on what they want. If you don't create the vision, things won't get done.

The Traits of a Leader

A number of personal traits enable a leader to really take charge of a team and generate results. In my view, the most important of these are as follows:

- Empathy
- Respect
- Empowerment
- Communication

- Commitment
- Vision
- Passion
- Optimism
- Integrity
- Service
- Honesty

How to Improve as a Leader

When you surround yourself either with a mentor who is very successful or within a mastermind group of people who are more successful than you, you will naturally come up to that level. The best analogy I can think of is when I was in track: if I ran against people who were faster than me, I would have a faster time myself because I was trying to keep up with them.

The other part of it is just being an avid reader—a lifelong learner—because there's a book out there for everything. Combining reading with getting that hands-on experience with a franchise or another type of business opportunity is vital, because there's nothing better than building your self-confidence and building your knowledge.

When you're a new leader or an existing leader, but especially when you're new, building a rapport with the staff and developing trust is the absolute foundation for everything. If they can't trust you, they're not going to come to you for anything.

Learning and Succeeding

To improve your chances of succeeding as a leader, be a lifelong learner. Always spend at least 10 percent of your time innovating and 10 percent of your time thinking outside the box and reinventing yourself. Think of alternative ways to do things because most people get blinders on and they're stuck. They can't get out of their own way. Self-development is absolutely crucial. Always ask yourself, "How do I get better?" I call it the Dream 50. Who are the people you most admire, such as business leaders, entrepreneurs, and successful CEOs, like Mark Zuckerberg and Warren Buffett? Regardless of what industry you're in, look at those avatars—who are actually real people—that you can try to emulate.

A lot of people emulate Elon Musk, Steve Jobs, Jeff Bezos, or Bill Gates. When you follow someone who is successful, like Steve Jobs, you are bound to learn tips on how they got there. You can use those tips to improve your plan. Ask yourself, "What have they done?" The truth in most cases is—and this is the funny part—they've simply taken action. There's a big joke about how you become successful, and there's a one-word answer: *start*. Do something.

For me, improvement all starts with creating a new daily routine. If you don't like what you're experiencing in your life, and you want more, get up earlier and stay up later. It starts with setting new goals, because the definition of insanity is doing the same thing over and over again and expecting different results. Create a new routine.

It goes back to "start." And that new routine helps answer, "What do I want in life?" And if it's being your own boss—that's usually a lot of what it is—then, for example, you could join various entrepreneurial Facebook groups. It's a safe environment to learn from other people. Read as much as you can. Get some of the top books on entrepreneurship and leadership to really immerse yourself in new content and learn more about what you specifically might be missing.

Modeling Success

There's an expression I use all the time, especially in franchising: "Model success." Franchising is all about that. You don't have to reinvent the wheel, but that expression goes to what my advice for people is: You need to model other people's success. So you follow Steve Jobs and see how he did it. Everybody's more comfortable following someone who is very successful, but the truth is there is nothing too surprising about how to develop your leadership skills other than getting out there and doing it and getting feedback.

Get 360-degree feedback. A lot of people talk about that. And it's exactly what I did with Karen. Get feedback from the people you respect. In my case, it was people I worked with: the best cook, the chef that ran the kitchen, or Karen the head food server. When you go to somebody you really respect and ask their opinion, boy, those are the people who give you the best advice.

Teach Confidence

Louis Columbus

Louis Columbus is an enterprise software leader, writer, and industry analyst with experience in marketing, product, sales, and strategic planning. His passion is creating and launching new enterprise applications, leading industry solutions teams and their go-to-market strategies. Previous positions include vice president, director, and senior management roles in various enterprise software and cloud computing companies and start-ups.

Mr. Columbus's academic background includes an MBA from Pepperdine University and Strategic Marketing Management, Digital Marketing, and Digital Value Chain Programs at Stanford University Graduate School of Business. In addition, Louis teaches MBA courses in international business, strategic planning, and market research. He is also currently a member of the faculty at Webster University and has taught at California State University Fullerton, University of California, Irvine & Marymount University. Mr. Columbus has also authored sixteen books on IT-related technologies.

Louis is also a columnist for several leading publications, including VentureBeat, *covering AI, cybersecurity, machine learning, and predictive analytics. Connect with Louis on LinkedIn to learn more.*

Growing Team Confidence Under Stress

How a team handles the stress of a new product launch says a lot about their current strengths, areas to improve, and confidence in themselves and the team overall. Leaders make or break a product launch with their decisions, such as who will be the cross-functional team lead. Realize that a product launch is, in many ways, a microcosm of launching a new business too.

The most experienced teams that know how to budget resources and coordinate product management and engineering, DevOps, marketing, and sales, still struggle. It's because core pieces of the software code get delayed, teams run behind, and product testing or QA finds new problems. In the meantime, competitors are also rushing products to market, including new cloud apps, web services, and next-generation products, to attract new customers. The pressure is on an entire team to deliver on time or ahead of schedule to meet market opportunities before competitors do.

It's admirable to see enterprise software companies achieve a steady cadence of new product launches—even throughout a pandemic. I have interviewed the leaders of DevOps, marketing, and product management teams who are achieving a steady, solid cadence of releases with well-executed launches. They all share a common series of traits, and their teams reflect a level of confidence earned from overcoming barriers and roadblocks while still producing excellent code and next-generation user experiences. The lessons learned from them—and my own experience—can help many leaders with struggling teams.

Just as launching products is a microcosm of launching a new business, the same holds for any leader's growth into their role through the launch process. Whether a product launch succeeds or not has a lot more to do with leaders first and their teams second. As a leader's effectiveness goes, so goes their team. It is common for enterprise software companies to see the best product management, marketing, and DevOps leaders get assigned to troubled launches. They are experts at turning teams around. Their leadership makes the difference from chronically missing dates and incomplete, buggy code with no interfaces to prototypes ready for testing in less than a month. In-demand leaders who turn projects around aren't pushing people to work harder. Instead, they have an innate ability to see where the constraints are, remove them, show confidence in the teams, and get them to believe in themselves again. Once confidence returns, productivity takes off, and everyone's stronger confidence helps to make the launch date attainable. Leaders with this innate skill to see confidence gaps and close them are in high demand. They get promoted and eventually end up in C-level positions in their careers. They are the kind of people who make you believe you can do anything. They also focus on getting team members beyond the Imposter Syndrome by learning new skills through doing.

Use Product Launches as a Catalyst to Close Confidence Gaps

Stressful events, including product launches, are useful for seeing where confidence gaps are and where you as a leader need to take action to close them. Product launches provide opportunities to grow as a leader. The following are key areas to concentrate on:

Team Goals and Launch Plans Supporting Them Need to Give Each Member a Chance to Excel

Your teams' productivity matters, but how they excel together is what matters most. And making this happen has to give each member of the team ownership of their outcomes—a chance to see that their contributions matter and make a difference. Look across your team, and you will see varying degrees of Imposter Syndrome. The first step in helping employees get beyond it is giving them a chance to own part of the launch and excel in their work. In creating team goals, consider how you can design them to eradicate Imposter Syndrome by giving every team member a chance to see that what they are doing counts.

Product Launches Are Also Learning and Proving Grounds

Product launches are a great opportunity for your team to learn new skills and get valuable feedback. One of the best ways to reduce Imposter Syndrome is to give every team member—especially those tending to doubt themselves and their ability—a chance to take on a challenging task that has a high-visibility payoff for the cross-functional team. Your job as their manager is to do everything you can to make sure they excel, giving them the support, training, and insights to turn the project into a win for them. That's a proven way to close confidence gaps and help your team get beyond Imposter Syndrome. Being completely committed to their success is essential.

Create and Strengthen Psychological Safety across the Team, Especially During Launches

Use product launches to strengthen the psychological safety of your team further. You're going to have some members on your team who are exceptional performers—the rock stars of the company. In some cases, they are in product management, and it's important to give them the freedom to excel and grow through a product launch. They are providing a model of what other team members can grow into. Give them a lot of autonomy, and you'll be amazed at what they accomplish. Rock stars are like anyone else, as they only thrive when there is psychological safety. It's also important to pay attention to those with Imposter Syndrome and those struggling and occasionally failing at tasks. In one-on-ones, letting them know this is all part of the learning process and that they are doing fine and are valued as a team member is essential. Stay focused on closing their confidence gaps so they grow into their roles. Helping them overcome Imposter Syndrome is part of what leading is all about.

Strive for Structural Stability and Shared Meaning for Your Team

A key part of closing confidence gaps and increasing overall team performance is staying true to the structure of your team and its meaning. The larger the organization, the more pressures there are to capitulate and try to have your team be all things to all people. Don't ever capitulate or compromise your team's sharing meaning or structure, especially in the middle of a launch. This is tantamount to having your team's back and not allowing any other department or team to change your goals and direction. Showing that resolve and strength will keep your team intact, preserve the progress you're making, keep confidence gaps shrinking, and keep your team together. Who wants to work for a boss who is always changing the direction and meaning of the department to try and please someone? No one does. Stay strong and committed to your team, and don't waiver.

Make Sure Every Team Member Knows What a First Victory Looks Like and How to Visualize It

One of the best books I've read on leadership recently is *The Confident Mind: A Battle-Tested Guide to Unshakable Performance* by Nate Zinsser.[5] I recommend it to anyone leading a team, department, or organization. Of the many valuable insights the book provides is the concept of what a First Victory is and why it's important to visualize them. Dr. Zinsser provides examples of how attaining First Victory drives greater self-confidence and closes confidence gaps. He also explains that self-confidence needs continual replenishing and that everyone needs to be on the lookout for what strengthens versus detracts from it. As a leader, you'll find the book invaluable for understanding how you can help your team members keep their self-confidence strong and growing. Best of all, the book helps to frame failure as one of the essential steps to

[5] Nate Zinsser, The Confident Mind: A Battle-Tested Guide to Unshakable Performance (New York City, NY: HarperCollins Publishers, 2022).

eventual success and describes how to avoid letting failures become roadblocks to attaining goals and leading teams.

Help Each Team Member Find Unique Strengths They Didn't Know They Had

I've always found this one of the most rewarding areas of managing and leading teams. I am also a strong believer in weekly one-on-ones, no matter where a team member or I am geographically. One-on-ones is where you help members of your team identify the unique strengths they have. While running a global cloud platform team, some of the best one-on-ones I had were with a rock star product manager who lives in Spain. We'd have one-one-ones while he traveled via train from his home to catch a flight or a customer meeting. I learned so much from him about how I could improve as a manager that the one-on-ones began helping me as much as they helped him. It also helped me see the innate strengths that he didn't have a chance to develop. For example, he has strong entrepreneurial instincts, which made him excel at product management and showed how he could easily run his own company someday. I encouraged him to think about starting a new business. He also had marketing skills he didn't have a chance to use that often. Fast-forward a few years, and he is running his own company, loves it, and is excelling in the industry he chose to compete in.

Don't Be Afraid to Enforce the No-Asshole Rule, Especially in the Middle of Tense Situations Like Product Launches

The most stressful situations bring out the worst in people, often seeing anger replace kindness. As a leader, you need to consider how the Stoics dealt with these challenges. One of the leading Stoics was Marcius Aurelius, a Roman emperor and philosopher. Marcus Aurelius wrote in *Meditations* that anger is weakness, and kindness is strength.[6] He compared people who get angry with animals who have no control or cognition of their behavior and how it impacts others. No doubt Marcus struggled with anger himself as he wrote about it so often. Another great book about managing difficult situations and people is *The No Asshole Rule: Building a Civilized Workplace and Surviving One That Isn't* by Bob Sutton.[7] The book's premise is that mean-spirited employees will sap the energy out of your team, create poor morale, and do their best to make the team fail. So don't think twice about getting rid of toxic employees who are harming your team and their confidence.

What Happens When Confidence and Skill Gaps Close

The most powerful words you can ever say to anyone on your team are "I believe in you." Back it up with a commitment to help them constantly improve and try never to miss a one-on-one. Your voice carries across the landscape of their lives much louder, longer, and with far-reaching impact than you could ever know. What they hear from you and the support you give them makes a difference in how they get along with peers, other company lead-

---

[6] Marcus Aurelius Antoninus, Meditations: Marcus Aurelius (Harmondsworth, Middlesex, England: Penguin Books, 1964).

[7] Robert I. Sutton, The No Asshole Rule: Building a Civilized Workplace and Surviving One That Isn't (New York City, NY: Business Plus, 2010).

ers, and, most importantly, their families. So why not invest the time and help them succeed and grow? It is the right thing to do from a leadership standpoint, and more importantly, from a human one. We're here to serve each other. Make it your goal as a leader that anyone who crosses your path as a member of your team emerges from the experience stronger, more capable of competing in a chaotic world—and most importantly, with confidence they can rely on to overcome the challenges coming their way. That's when leadership becomes most rewarding. Years later, you may get a call from one of them thanking you for your support as they tell you they beat out dozens of other candidates to win a new C-level position they never believed they could achieve. Be the leader who helps each member of your team reach new heights in their career.

Leadership as a Legacy

Johnny Marines

A native New Yorker from the Lower East side, Johnny Marines played a huge part in the meteoric rise to fame of the Latin American group Aventura and global Bachata star Romeo Santos. Prior to his career in the music business, Johnny started out as an NYPD police officer, eventually rising to the rank of sergeant. During the course of his career with NYPD, he was awarded twelve Excellent Police Duty medals. For his work helping Romeo Santos's career, Johnny was selected three times as one of the 30 most influential people in Latin music by Billboard.

Johnny has never lost sight of his roots. He has devoted significant time and resources to giving back to the community, including helping to create and fund a nonprofit sports academy and establishing the Johnny Marines Blessings Foundation to support educational advancement initiatives within New York City.

More recently, Johnny has become a serial entrepreneur, owning several nightlife/restaurant venues. He is also a real estate investor and tech investor who serves as a strategic partner for several tech startup companies. Additionally, he serves on the advisory board of the music app Trubify and the alcohol beverage company Ya Ve Tequila.

Leadership as a Legacy

I think I demonstrated leadership abilities early on as a child. I know I was definitely learning them at the time. I was heavily influenced by my father, an entrepreneur, when I was a kid. Although maybe at the moment it didn't seem like I was going to go into entrepreneurship because all I ever wanted to do was be a police officer—which I ended up doing and am now a retired NYPD sergeant. Along the way, I went into the music business and, from there, I started to branch out into entrepreneurship.

I've been given the privilege of having a managerial or supervisory position in the roles I've occupied through the years, first when I became a police officer and then became a sergeant. That was my first experience of having a position at a managerial level. I was in charge of a certain number of cops and what they were doing. From there, I went on to manage a very famous group, a Latin band called Aventura. I did that for some time, and then they split up.

Then I started managing the lead singer from the group, Romeo Santos. And in that field, being a manager requires you to really be on top of things, because there are a lot of moving pieces in the music industry. It's a pretty heavy task to take on, especially when the artist is really big, like Romeo Santos. But that also allowed me to grow in my mindset of how to be able to run a business, because an artist is like a business, in a way. So if you look at an artist like a business, I was able to take that experience and transfer over what I learned from being in a managerial position and the music business. When I finally got my first business, I had the experience of knowing how to deal with employees.

Leadership and Challenges

In my career, I've always been, more or less, in a position of leadership. That leadership allows me to be able to manage whatever I have in front of me, whether it's artists or my own businesses, while also giving me the opportunity to teach the employees, because that's what leadership is about. Leadership is not about telling people what to do; it's about the people you are leading and learning from the experience. When you're able to teach your personnel rather than just instruct them, the value of that employee becomes so much greater. Because now you have someone who knows the business, not only do they have an opportunity to move up in your business, where you could turn an employee into a manager, but they also have the ability to own their own business in the future. That's how you create leaders.

As a leader, I've never looked at anything as a struggle. I only look at things as challenges. But I also look at every challenge as if it can be won. And the thing about dealing with challenges and lessons that you learn any time you're in a position of leadership is that a lot of times when you get challenged, it brings out the best in you. It makes you work harder, it makes you want to accomplish things, and it brings out the best person that you can actually be at that moment. And this will allow you to be an even better leader. You will learn how to take on challenges, not give up, not quit and make excuses, but rather find a way to overcome whatever challenges you face.

I think one of the biggest mistakes that I've seen people make is to give up, because they feel like they failed. The truth is, there's no failing, only life lessons. You have to take the lessons that you get taught and then convert what you learned and turn them into a positive. If you're able to do that, rather than get frustrated and just give up, realize that's what makes great leaders, and that's what makes successful people. So many people give up. That's why there are so many people who don't live out their dreams in life.

Leading by Example

I think my leadership style is one where I like to lead by example. I don't like to tell people to do things that I'm not willing to do myself. At the same time, I'm a very understanding leader, and I try to give people opportunities—even when they make mistakes, because I also remember when I made mistakes. So I'm able to take those experiences and use myself as an example, to then be a better leader. When somebody makes a mistake, I like to address the mistake and then simply explain to them how they can correct it moving forward.

I've always been a patient leader. I think that's where we win—when a leader shows patience and does not react impulsively. I don't believe in being impulsive because from what I've learned after being around people who are impulsive, they don't necessarily make the best decisions for themselves or the company. The way I like to lead is by taking a step back and looking at my options and weighing them before I make an impulsive decision that might not necessarily be great for the company.

I motivate people by letting them know that there's always a chance to grow within the company. I can show them people who are now in managerial positions, who worked under me and were once lower-level employees, who I saw had the desire to want to grow and learn. And

I was able to notice those people and the amount of work they were putting in. I gave them not just a pat on the back but also raised them to a position I felt comfortable they could handle and would be good for the company. When they see people who started in their position now being their boss, they know that they also have an opportunity to grow in the company.

The Values of a Leader

There's been no one particular event that I could point out that could say, "This happened to me, and it completely made me change." I think I just looked at everything that I was doing and understood that I wasn't going to get everything right. There is no one event that has occurred to me that has made me change who I am or how I viewed things; for me, it's just kind of learn as you go.

I believe the values a leader should have are patience and honesty. Teach, and lead by example. I think these are the things that when somebody works underneath you and see these values in you, they're going to respect you as a leader. The one thing that I like to point out—because I've seen different types of leaders—is that there are leaders who are feared, and there are leaders who are respected. And the respected leaders still get the job done, but people will enjoy doing it for that leader. And when you do it for somebody you respect, you do it with passion and love. There's a big difference there, and it shows.

What It Takes to Be a Leader

To be a successful leader and run a successful company or organization is key. Yes, everything starts at the top, and if you're not organized at the top, you're not going to be organized at the bottom level. And your day-to-day people who are running your company need to be pointed in the right direction. There needs to be a plan in place that is effective and that your employees can respect and actually implement. One of the worst things that I've seen at companies is disorganization. Being disorganized at a company can lead to an unavoidable crash and burn.

It's true that sometimes disorganization has to happen first before you actually get organized, because sometimes you think you're organized, but you're not as organized as you thought you were. All of a sudden, it can lead to some disorganization and point out the flaws in your plan. I'm the type of guy where, if there is disorganization somewhere, you can call me to come and clean up that mess, because I will point out all your mistakes and all your flaws and everything that's being done wrong.

Success is measured by results. And it is not only the numbers, just to clear that up. Results are everything; it does have to do with numbers, but it also has to do with how we get to those numbers. There are a lot of steps to get to the numbers. They don't just appear magically.

If I had a chance to do it all over again, I wouldn't change a thing, because everything that I learned along the way—the good, the bad, the failures, the successes—is what made me who I am today. Without experiencing both ends of the stick, I wouldn't be able to be an effective leader. Because the thing is, everybody is scared to fail in life. But the truth is that failure is probably the best thing that can happen to you, because you're going to learn more from failing than you can ever learn from being successful.

If I was successful in everything I did from day one, I wouldn't really appreciate it; I wouldn't even care or be scared to go backwards. Without going through those bad moments, you cannot appreciate being successful. Life is like a roller coaster. It goes up, and it goes down. That goes for everybody. I don't care how famous or rich you are.

Believe in Yourself

You have to believe in yourself, and you have to finish everything that you start—you can't leave things halfway done. If you start it, you finish it. Use the people who don't believe in you as motivation for that chip on your shoulder; use them as that fuel to the fire—even if you've got to make them up, and they're fictitious, and there's nobody rooting against you. They can create this drive within you, this desire to prove them wrong. And you can translate that into something positive.

Life is crazy—because as you get older, you get fewer and fewer people rooting for you. This is real; maybe it's because you get to be part of the competition, or, people just don't like to see other people doing better than they are. It's the total opposite of when you're a kid, because when you're a kid, and you get up, and you start to walk, and everybody sees you in that living room, and they're thinking, "Oh my God, look at Johnny. He just stood up. He's walking!" And everybody's cheering you on.

Well, when you get older, that cheering doesn't go on too often. So you have to be able to deal with pushing yourself. You have to make use of your drive to take it to the next level, and you have to be able to block out the noise. Sometimes you can't do everything yourself, because to be an effective leader, you need a strong team to move the company forward.

When you want to give up, sometimes it's because you're trying to do too much. You're by yourself. You think you're the one who has to know everything. One of my strengths has always been to pair myself up with people who I feel are at the same level as me. I was never afraid, and I'm not afraid now to pair myself up with somebody who knows a lot more than I do.

The reason I actually like them knowing more than me is I know I can learn from them. Imagine if every time you walked into a room, you were the smartest person in the room. What information could you possibly leave the room with? None. But now, if you walk into a room where there are several people who know more than you, you're in a position to learn and to leave that room with something.

I'll just end by saying my advice for people when they want to quit is one word: no.

A Holistic Approach to Pricing Power

Per Sjöfors

Per Sjöfors authored The Price Whisperer: A Holistic Approach to Pricing Power.[8] *He's also a member of the Forbes Magazine Business Council, a member of the C-Suite Network, appears regularly on podcasts and business radio shows, and has been quoted repeatedly in the financial press, including* Inc. *magazine,* TheStreet, Fortune *magazine,* Industry Week, Business Insider, *and the* Financial Times. *More about his business can be found at* https://sjofors.com.

How I Became the Price Whisperer

The German autobahn outside Stuttgart, Germany, is straight but goes over several small hills, so the visible distance is limited. This rainy, dark late Friday on a November afternoon, around 6 p.m., visibility was even more limited. I came over the top of one of these small hills and could see, just in front of me, three cars that collided and were still spinning around on the wet surface. Somehow, I managed to avoid all three still-spinning cars while driving over the crushed glass and other debris. Then, as I tried to swallow my heart, I looked in the rearview mirror and saw the silhouettes of the three cars in front of a wall of light and smoke. It took me some time to realize

[8] Per Sjöfors, The Price Whisperer: A Holistic Approach to Pricing Power (New York City, NY: Leaders Press, 2022).

the smoke was from the tires of cars that tried to stop to avoid the collided cars. Unsuccessfully. There were about a hundred cars in the consequent pileup, and several people perished. The autobahn was closed for at least twenty-four hours. My car was the only one that got through.

So what was I, a native Swede, doing on the German autobahn? Well, I was on the way home to Zürich, Switzerland, from a business meeting somewhere in Germany. I had relocated to Zurich a few years earlier when my then-boss presented his most significant challenge to me:

- Establish a new company (which I had never done).
- Be the CEO of the new company (something I had never been).
- Build that company into an international powerhouse with customers across Europe (which I had never done).

All of this was in Zürich, in a language and culture I did not know. I was scared out of my wits. And equally excited!

It was in this company I got my first practical lesson in pricing. The company I established was a manufacturers' rep organization. We represented manufacturers, set up a network of national distributors, and promoted their products, but the manufacturers sold directly to the distributors, and we earned a commission on their sales. We started the company by representing a single US-based manufacturer and eventually represented a handful of non-European professional electronics manufacturers in the European market. That first manufacturer had invented a significantly lower-cost way of manufacturing a device that was equal in quality to the market leader and more feature-rich. As a rep org, we did not control pricing, and the US manufacturer had decided that the product should be significantly lower in price than that market leader, and this low-price strategy led to several things:

With a price about half that of the market leader, the dollar margin for the device was very low, and as a result, the manufacturer always struggled. They never had enough resources for product development, and it took ages for new and enhanced products to be available. Likewise, insufficient resources were available to market the products, and customer support was sub-par.

With a low price from the manufacturer, the distributors marked up the devices significantly, making considerably more money than the manufacturer or my rep firm. I was exposed to numerous conversations with potential customers who doubted we could deliver quality on par with the market leader.

For consequent manufacturers we represented, I could influence their pricing, and together with our national distributors, we conducted pricing experiments, always trying to hone in on that one "optimal" price.

With my success in Switzerland supporting me, the next several career moves felt equally exciting, but no less intimidating. I was recruited to become the CEO of the London-based European subsidiary of a Japanese electronics manufacturer. I did not know what to expect in terms of cultural differences, as I was used to Europe and US cultures. But it turned out it was a lot easier than I thought. It was all about being open, honest, and humble, and I never had any kind of culture clash with Japan. Despite a deep recession, business was good, and I managed to quadruple European revenue over three years.

The next step in my journey started on a Florida highway. As I was driving, I looked around and said to myself, "Maybe I should move to the US." So I took myself and my wife, who had been with me from Sweden to Switzerland and the UK, across the pond to Los Angeles, where I joined a large public company to run a newly established division. I grew it from zero to eight figures over a couple of years. Here I did find an unexpected culture clash. Despite working with a legion of US-based companies over the years, I had worked *with* these companies, not *in* them. I did not realize the need to constantly "sell" myself internally. I was used to having the results speak for themselves. Not so here. I also found the company fear-driven. Many staff members worked hard to protect themselves, making short-term decisions for their own "safety," sometimes to the company's detriment. I've seen some odd decision behavior from some US companies over the years. I now realize this also stemmed from fear within the companies, where individuals made decisions to guard their backs and not for the company's benefit.

After holding several more CEO positions in various companies where we continued doing pricing experiments, the conclusion was that some of these worked spectacularly well. For example, the subsequent quarter's revenue increased by 25 percent, but many experiments failed. However, to find the reason why many experiments failed, I found that business schools' teachings and books about pricing were too abstract and too academic for a business executive to act on. It was just useless information.

Consequently, having experienced both successful and not-so-successful pricing experiments, I set out to make pricing practical and actionable—to define a process that would have given me the necessary answers to make every pricing experiment successful. The answer was to develop a process and a holistic view of a company and its pricing, realizing that everything a company does affects what pricing strategy it can adopt. And then we could build a company around that process. Since then, I have been at the forefront as a pricing thought leader, taking an untraditional view on everything regarding pricing.

Having confidence in myself, I decided to make my company virtual from day one. (I hate commuting. Such a waste of time—and money.) This was fifteen years ago, long before virtual companies were common. Building a virtual company meant that I had to recruit self-motivated staff who could work without supervision and deliver the results I wanted—obviously, individuals who, like me, don't want to be told what to do.

Leading in an Open Environment

When it comes to leadership, I believe it comes naturally to some people and that leadership training and coaching can improve a good leader but can never make a nonnatural leader successful. In my case, as a teenager and young adult, I remember that when I was with my friends, we almost always ended up watching the movies I wanted to see and going to the restaurants, bars, and discos (yes, I know I age myself here) that I wanted to visit. So I naturally led my group of friends.

Furthermore, I recall that when in the military, the routine bored me to death, and I ended up volunteering for anything that broke up the routine. I had a tremendous appetite to learn new things and find and overcome new challenges. This also means I'm prepared to take risks, learn, and have new experiences. Being prepared to take risks is crucial to any leader. Without risk, there is no reward. If you are not prepared to take a risk, someone else will, leaving your company in the dust.

I guess one measure of my management style and the results I generated in these various companies is that I have never been fired. I've never been on the receiving end of that awkward conversation that starts with, "This is not working out."

As a leader, my approach has always been transparency, honesty, and inclusiveness. The result is that employees have repeatedly told me I was their best boss. I have even become personal friends with employees—some after I fired them!

What I mean by transparency is simply to be open about the company's situation—what is good and bad—and to share the goals I see for the company. Honesty obviously plays into that. Praise staff when appropriate, and criticize when appropriate. Inclusiveness, for me, means two things: first, include staff in critical decisions that may affect the company; second, present staff with a vision and goals and allow them to figure out how to reach these goals. The result is a sense of ownership and responsibility among staff members. The flip side is that staff members who do not subscribe to the company's vision or want to be told what to do are the wrong kind of staff members and need to be ejected quickly—one bad apple, etc.

I also believe recruitment many times is done the wrong way. I've always been aghast seeing recruitment ads that have a page or two of "requirements." For me, it is about hiring the most brilliant, passionate, and driven people, and if you do, they "will figure it out." So in the open environment I have created, if staff think they need advice, want to be mentored, or want training, they simply find sources for advice, mentoring, or training. These come from sources that rarely are from me and most often come from third parties. They figure it out because they, just like me, own the company's vision and are engaged in their role and the company. Consequently, I firmly believe that any kind of staff betterment needs to come from staff members themselves. (We obviously conduct all training that's required by law.)

For me, creating that open, honest environment is absolutely crucial, and to be able to do so, a leader needs confidence in their own ability and position. Be open to taking criticism from staff, who also feel they can do so with confidence and without risk of having their career path damaged or becoming persecuted in any way. I think this is really important, because if the right team is hired, they will often have better answers than you.

I found it "funny" when the pandemic hit, and we all had to take our companies virtual (mine already was, as I mentioned), and in the various networking groups I attend, I could see some CEOs incredibly frustrated as they could no longer micromanage their direct reports. It was a failure in my mind, both by the CEOs who micromanaged and the staff who allowed it to happen.

In closing, what have I learned on my leadership journey? Well, in addition to what's above, a few more things stand out: First, a leader needs to lead by example. If you want staff with a strong work ethic, you need to have a strong work ethic. If you want honest staff, you need to be honest. Furthermore, I believe you must be friendly and accessible, but not friends with your staff. As a leader, it is essential to realize that they often know better than you. Finally, you must admit you are a leader not because you know but because you know how to find out!

More about my speaking activity can be found here at https://www.persjofors.com, and to find my latest book, just search for the book title *The Price Whisperer*.

Achieve to Lead

Fadwa AlBawardi

*Ms. Fadwa Saad AlBawardi is a Saudi Arabian entrepreneur who have established her own consultancy office in KSA (*https://fsab.sa.com*) in order to provide consulting services in Digital Transformation and its strategies, including AI strategies, Business Intelligence, Data Governance, Digital Economy, and Strategic Planning.*

Ms. AlBawardi's entrepreneurship efforts aim to help individuals (researchers and academics), as well as private and governmental sector organizations, to build their strategic plans and improve their strategic and operational performance through identifying and analyzing key issues, provide recommendations to resolve them, as well as plan KPIs/OKRs to monitor performance progress.

Ms. AlBawardi is a Certified Strategy and Business Planning Professional, as well as an Information Technology and Performance Management Senior Consultant, with more than twenty-one years of working experience. Ms. AlBawardi earned a master's degree in Computer Science from Boston University, a bachelor's degree in Computer Science from the American University (Cairo), a Strategic Planning course from Harvard University, and has been awarded two strategic planning certificates (UAE).

Signs of a Leader

I believe that I had leadership qualities since I was young. Even as a girl, maybe eleven or twelve years old, when I traveled with my parents, I always noticed in the airport that I liked to take charge of my own things. For example, I always insisted on holding my own passport and showing it to the passport officer myself. I remember this very well, because my family was very surprised at this. At work, I do like to have my own freedom to think and have my own freedom to act. I'm not very happy when people try to dictate that I take a certain direction.

When I was younger as well, I was always looking for a field of study that I thought would lead to a good future. I chose the IT field because I envisioned it to be in constant demand. Everybody needs it because it's a field of the present and the future.

I've recently started my own consulting office. I felt the time was right, having already worked for more than twenty-one years in the field. I've had good experiences in IT, so I took the next step and started my own business. I started being a leader at work, probably five years after I began working. In the beginning, I was just part of the team. My superiors saw something in me, so I was assigned the role of a team leader, then a manager, then a director, and then I became a senior consultant.

Facing Challenges as a Leader

There are certain challenges in any workplace, especially when dealing with people. Managing people is one of the toughest jobs in business. When you are managing people, you have to keep a number of things in perspective: how to balance emotional intelligence with actually doing things the way that they should be done as well as how to make sure you are showing a certain amount of strength in addition to being supportive.

It's this kind of balance that is so challenging to get right. For example, if there is a coworker who is very lazy or doesn't want to do a task, not because of a lack of time, but just because he or she doesn't want to do it, you need to deal with this situation in a way that doesn't ruin the relationship with that person, but at the same time gets things done in a professional manner.

To overcome such situations, communication is key. I usually talk to the person, in my office or over coffee, and explain that we need more from each other—we need them to work harder and deliver on time. When necessary, I offer support by asking questions in order to try to understand the situation better. However, if it turns out in the end that they don't want to work just for the sake of it, because they think somebody else is going to do the work for them, that is not acceptable. In that case, things have to be a bit more official. You need to ask them to provide their work by a certain time, and if they don't, then you need to put it in an official email. Usually, when you reach that point, they will respond. Therefore, it's a step that you should try to avoid until absolutely necessary. However, sometimes as a leader, you do need to take strict action.

Delegate to Avoid Micromanaging

As a leader, I'm very supportive. I'm very understanding. I like to empower people to help them reach their potential. At the same time, I make sure that this is not perceived as weakness or softness. It is actually eagerness on my side to be part of the team, not as a leader per se, not as a superior, but to be one of them as much as possible. This approach has been a big help to me during my career. It has led to keeping me in communication with many people I've worked with even after we were no longer coworkers.

I like to delegate. I hate micromanagement since I think it's exhausting for everybody. It's exhausting to the leader and the team members who don't feel trusted when leaders take this approach. I like people to take responsibility. At the same time, I like to acknowledge people for what they do. I very much like sending appreciation letters. If somebody does something praiseworthy, like doing a great job in a big role in a project, I like to officially commend them so that the team can see they have done something extra, and that they have helped us achieve our goals. I believe that, from an emotional standpoint, this helps them achieve even more in their next assignments.

I think I have always been a supportive leader because this is part of my nature. However, being this type of leader has not stopped me from achieving goals. For example, some people have asked to be transferred to my team because they were comparing the different styles of leadership, and they thought mine was more understanding, encouraging, and closer to the team. Even my superiors have noticed this, which increased their trust in me and led them to assign me more and bigger projects.

I aim to motivate people first by very explicitly explaining the objectives. What are we trying to achieve? How will this benefit us? There is a career path that I usually discuss with HR for my team so that everybody knows exactly what the expected path is. They know that if they do well, even if they don't get promotions, at least they will make progress horizontally. I also explain to them that they will be gaining a lot of recognition and experience, especially with the delegation and the trust in them to do the job.

The Courage of a Leader

When I was in my first job, I attended a big meeting where our superior, the chairman, was reluctant to accept the project idea that my manager proposed. He was very doubtful, thinking that maybe this project was not doable for technical reasons. I remember I was very enthusiastic about the project, so I raised my hand, even though I was still one of the junior staff, and told the chairman, "It's doable. And I can prove it to you. After one week, you will get a prototype."

When I said that, even my manager looked at me as if to say, "Can you really do it?" And then I went back to the office and talked with the rest of the team. Working together, we had a prototype ready after one week, and we showed it to the chairman, and he was very happy. In that same meeting, he said to everybody, "I'm giving you the green light. It's accepted. We can go ahead with the project since this prototype shows that it actually can be done."

What I learned from this is that you need to have the courage to step up. If you believe in something, you cannot be passive or let people change your mind. Sometimes, when you face hesitance from people who are of a higher authority and power, it makes you doubt, at least a little bit, your own thinking. However, this shouldn't sway you. Sometimes powerful people need you to show them that things can be done at the granular level. After learning that, I became more open about expressing my opinions and points of view in meetings.

The Characteristics of a Leader

To be a leader, I believe you need to be very passionate about what you do and very supportive of the people who are working with you. You need to have the quality of being resilient. Sometimes things don't go smoothly. Sometimes there are pitfalls. Sometimes there are mistakes. However, when they occur, ask yourself, "How can you raise yourself up again? How can you succeed?" Having self-confidence is also very important in order to be a leader, because if you are weak or show a lack of confidence, the people around you will not be confident in you. I think it's important to be humble; however, you need to be self-confident as well. They are not mutually exclusive attitudes.

Problem-solving is crucial to success. Critical thinking and assessing risks/issues are also very important leadership skills. Adding to all that: emotional intelligence and strategic planning as well as the technical knowledge that a leader needs in order to run the business.

A leader needs to be very smart. I know sometimes they rely on people who work with them in order to find solutions to problems. However, it's also vital for the leader to have the wisdom to evaluate the suggestions and recommendations that they are given and pick the right one.

As a leader, waking up early is important to achieving your goals, because you can accomplish a lot in the morning. I also think that having a healthy lifestyle is vital: getting out and walking, maybe to enjoy nature or have the chance to just sit in a garden or a park to clear your mind.

It's very important to be compassionate and to be passionate about your own work. This is a key thing. Once you are passionate about what you want to do, and you build this compassion with the people who work with you, I think you have it all.

Success and Failure as a Leader

I believe that success happens when you reach your objectives, whether it's short term or long term. If you are looking for financial gain or for professional/career gain, either could qualify as a success objective. Some people think that failure is when you don't achieve your objectives, which is definitely part of it, but not all of it. Sometimes you meet your objectives; however, something goes wrong in the process, and then you feel that even though everybody sees that you have succeeded, you would think, "No, I have failed somehow." For example, if you had a major conflict with a co-worker or a partner, and they told you, "Okay, fine, we'll do that. However, I'm never going to work with you again." Even though you have technically succeeded in reaching your objective, you have failed in maintaining this work relationship, which is considered a loss. For me, failure is when you lose an asset that is important—whether it's an objective, a career partner, or a coworker—it just depends on how you define failure.

If I could do it again, I don't think I would do things differently, because in every leadership position or managerial position, I have learned a lot, and I wouldn't have excelled in the next step unless I had the experience from the previous situation. For me, it's been a journey of experiences, some involving mistakes that I learned from, others involving successes that I'm very proud of.

How to Be a Better Leader

I would advise a leader to start with having a mission and a vision first; it's essential for the leader to have the vision to know exactly what they want to accomplish by the end of the year, after three years, five years, or even ten years.

It's also vital to know how you can achieve your strategic objectives based on this vision and have the means to measure your progress closely.

I would also advise a leader to be very open to change. I believe that you need to be adaptable. Sometimes you need to be flexible and look at things from a different point of view. I think good leaders have this way of looking at things from all different sides so they can determine the best angle to tackle subjects or issues.

Change management needs to be both top-down and bottom-up. For example, if you have plans to improve the organization, you cannot really do that without getting support and buy-in from your superiors. Therefore, the way that you need to approach change management is either to keep it just for your section or team or for the whole organization. In both cases, you need a valid plan that people buy into.

If a person is hired for a certain position, I very much believe in agility. I believe that people can always do more if given the opportunity. Even though they were hired for a specific position, I tend to give them the opportunity to attend meetings that perhaps they are not really entitled to at their level. However, I like them to learn other roles in order to help broaden their understanding, because some people can actually be very creative. They can come up with brilliant ideas that improve the organization's ability to achieve its objectives if given the opportunity, empowerment, and support.

Aligning on Purpose, Mission, and Vision

Stephanie Crowe

Stephanie Crowe helps leaders multiply their people's performance for 10x ROI. She strongly believes that it is people who power businesses, and she helps them achieve their goals by identifying and revealing often hidden paths to business success. Steph is the leader of the Worldline group's learning, development, and transformation efforts.

She utilizes creative learning methods to connect the dots for talent globally, helping people feel aligned and fired up so they can multiply their impact.

Prior to joining Worldline, Steph held several senior-level global learning and development roles and founded her own learning company. She started her career as a principal consultant for PricewaterhouseCoopers. Steph helps organizations make the most of their greatest asset: their people. She has helped people and organizations convert what are perceived as business roadblocks into tremendous opportunities for over twenty years. Her strategy is to use an integrated approach to holistically evaluate a company—its challenges and opportunities—in order to identify the clearest and most direct path to overcoming barriers and properly aligning personnel with organizational objectives. She earned her bachelor's degree in International Studies from American University and received an MBA from The Wharton School, graduating with honors from both institutions.

It's all fun and games until somebody learns something!

Learning as a Superpower and Leading Change for Good

I believe that people power business and that extraordinary things can be accomplished when we unlock the talents people are gifted with and align them with mission and purpose. I've seen this occur time and again in my career, and it's my mission to help organizations and people discover their unique talents and use them to impact the world in positive ways.

Unlocking Your Gifts

My first discovery as a leader was to figure out how to play to my strengths. Underutilized talent exists everywhere, and leaders must tune into their own strengths and simultaneously give people the opportunity to unlock theirs.

On my early journey, I feel like I tried all the jobs. I picked blueberries by the bucket and manned the salad bar at the local pizza joint. I answered the phones and dialed for dollars, configured the technology system, designed training classes, and taught them. At one point, I ran the diskette duplication machine and packaged and sealed packs of diskettes (yes, that used to be a thing). I managed a restaurant and ran promotions to get more customers in on the weekends. I grew up with a firm belief that anything I wanted to do, I could learn. And so I did.

Learning how to do all these jobs did two important things for me: It increased my learning speed while expanding my breadth of awareness on what it takes for the world to function. It also helped me discover what I was good at along with what I hated. This is so important because so many people spend their lives trying to do what other people tell them they should rather than trying a whole lot of things to discover their strengths and joys.

At one of those odd jobs—working a salad bar at the local pizza restaurant—I met a friendly and talented young woman who taught me how to do the job. Janine was friendly, planful, and organized and always made sure the right things got done, at the right time, with efficiency and a smile. This was a summer job for me, so when I got a call from a friend asking if I'd like to help her dad's dentist's office part-time, I declined, knowing I'd soon be busy with my high school studies and after-school activities. But something made me think of Janine. I called back my friend and recommended her, who turned out to be an excellent fit for the role and eventually ended up pursuing higher education and a long and happy career in dentistry.

Later, when putting myself through school, I took a job on campus in a program office part-time. It seemed to me the process could be automated, so I built a database and a wizard, documented it, taught others how to do it, and moved on to another job. That's just how my mind works, and I enjoy looking at systems and improving them. Eventually, I followed this strength and went into consulting, and this way of thinking led me to Learning & Development and eventually leadership in this field.

Influence—It's All Fun and Games

One of the most important parts of the leader's role is to lead people through change, which requires influence. When people have fun, they are more open to learning and more open to influence. All learning is change, and all positive change requires learning. So it follows that leadership is at least a little bit about fun and games! I'll share what I mean by that.

Technology companies often go through leaps of discontinuous change. At one point, I was brought into a major software company to help move the organization from a siloed product set to an integrated one, which meant everyone had to understand everyone else's area of expertise, at least enough for the solution to work fully end-to-end. To lead through this change, we designed a game where the learners "build" the pieces of the end-to-end solution and then run scenarios through the whole solution, getting points for good choices and losing them for poor ones. Sure, it was learning, but it was also fun. The insights from the game produced major positive impacts on the employees, the solutions they designed, and the customer experience. It created the environment for collaboration since teams now understood the value and impact of each other's piece of the puzzle.

On another occasion, I had the opportunity to work with a retailer whose distribution centers weren't operating well. They knew the warehouses should be able to support two to three times as much volume, but the workers were untrusting of the managers, and no one could see the whole picture except the leaders. We co-designed a game where the employees played their way through a gameboard representing the warehouse, expediting the movement of goods, getting penalties for team errors with safety or processes, and the teams could celebrate at the end by completing tasks together like sealing trucks for shipment. Not only did the game help each person in the warehouse see the "whole picture" that previously only the leader could see, but it also simulated the teamwork necessary for them to work together efficiently.

Why is this leadership? Because it's the leader's role to create an environment for success. Not all leadership and change solutions must be fully designed games, of course. And you can have fun in simple ways and build teams during that fun. In my experience, people break down their barriers through games and create an environment for collaboration. As a leader, if you create a positive environment of fun, you also create an environment that allows for success.

The Self-Aware Leader

The most dangerous things for leaders as they grow are blind spots, and like any leader, I am no exception. The only way to overcome blind spots is to solicit feedback—often and authentically.

My earliest leadership experiences were in high school, where I led several clubs and teams, from the Future Business Leaders of America to the Key Club to the Drama Club. For the most part, the student members didn't want the leadership role: "Just tell us, and we'll do it." At this stage, leadership was more about having the drive on figuring out how to get things done. When I got to the working world, I had a very different experience.

After university, I pursued consulting, where I started on global projects quite quickly, working in teams to get collaborative outcomes with the client. I did my first facilitation in my early twenties, with a bunch of very smart and very senior people, as we were challenged to solve a complex many-tiered problem. I was so interested in "performing" the facilitation correctly that I very nearly told them what to think.

This, of course, is neither encouraging nor influential. I still remember the feedback I received when I asked how I did. I was praised for a good outcome, and the facilitation had progressed successfully with great ideas, but some of the team felt that I had been "condescending." Essentially, they were saying that I was telling them how things should go. I was being a teacher and teaching people things instead of facilitating these smart people and letting things flow, letting their intelligence figure things out. When I started working with other leaders and people who are good at and passionate about their jobs, they didn't like just being told what to do, and they didn't want a preconceived decision before they'd had a chance to give input.

I was holding on too tight versus creating the dynamics for good work to flow. You also can't let go completely and say, "Let me know when you get there." That's not leadership. For me, the best approach is to know what the necessary structural elements are so you can say, "Here's where we're going. Here are the tools you need. Let's get there together."

Collaborative leadership is one of the most difficult, yet most rewarding, forms of leadership. Teams and other leaders are motivated because they are involved and invested in the collective outcome, and there is little to no concern of "credit" or "control" because the whole team owns the result. And of course, the research backs this up. Multiple brains, especially of different kinds, solving a problem produce better outcomes that one in isolation or even several in a chain.

Improving as a Leader: Learning

Leadership is a verb. To continue to lead, leaders must commit to growth, development, and focus. But where to start? The path to leadership is knowing yourself. Get to know your superpower, and you'll get to know who you are as a leader. Ask for feedback, and then commit to learning and growing. Every leader should have their own learning plan. This is not an easy road, but it is intrinsically rewarding. I've personally always been committed to excellence, but excellence looks a lot different for leaders than it does for individual contributors.

As a student, I was always focused on getting the "A" and that "Good job!" from the teacher. When I moved into the work world, naturally, I focused on building excellent work products so I could continue to get that recognition. To move from being a consultant and trainer to being a manager, I had to focus on being a good manager by coaching and supporting my team to do the training, instructional development, and consulting work. To be an effective director, I had to be a leader for the training managers, regional advisors, and operations team and focus on working with stakeholders and customers and not take over their work, which would be both distracting for me and insulting to them.

For achievers who have become leaders, this is a tough transition to make. To be a leader is to give the recognition, not to get it, so over time, you have to wean yourself from the need for external validation and steer instead to the intrinsic rewards of the team achieving the mission.

Improving as a Leader: Focus

To be a lasting leader, you must be committed to continuous learning. And leaders must be relentless in their focus. Focus is in short supply these days, and that is by no means less of an issue for leaders. You cannot spend time and energy on things that are not aligned with your purpose and mission. But time is not a zero-sum game, because some things give you energy and others deplete it. You have to maximize the things that give you energy and delegate the things that do not.

Throughout my life, I have worn many hats, and we should all recognize that leaders are also mothers and fathers, siblings, caregivers, friends, community members—the list goes on. When my children were young, I looked at my time and tried to logically plan how I could spend enough of it working, taking care of the home, and taking care of the family. Eventually, we hired a part-time nanny so I could focus on work when the kids were not at school or daycare. But what really ended up happening was that I found myself taking some of that extra time to get the house back into shape after a disastrous day or week—catching up on dishes, laundry, and the like—which are not my strengths. I'm embarrassed to say that I did not predict what may be obvious now. It finally occurred to me one day while I was pushing myself to get laundry done, and hating it, as I saw the nanny playing outdoors with my kids. What had I done?! I realized that it would be better to delegate the home care and save for myself the joy of spending time with my kids even if child rearing was a set of new skills I needed to learn—they were skills and experiences I wanted and would reap benefits for a lifetime.

The easy way to go about focusing your time and energy is to make a list of the things you do every day and put a plus or minus next to each to mark whether it gives you energy or takes it away. Then persistently and consistently identify the things that take away your energy and delegate them. Because if you're always spending time on things that are draining you, there's no way you will get more time or energy to spend on the things that you should be doing and growing your talents and growing your leadership. If it's not aligned with your purpose, then delegate it or start saying no. Overcommitting yourself and your team will demotivate your team, and they will no longer trust you. So you need to know what to say no to.

Mission, Vision, and Purpose

Many people seem to think that leaders are in their position because they know, and tell people, WHAT to do. In truth, the most important part of leadership is to know WHY. Leaders must clearly define the **mission** for the organization towards an inspirational future **vision** that rests solidly within its **purpose**—the reason the organization exists. Why does the company exist? Why should the team rally all their strength, skill, and intellect to execute the mission? What's so important about it, and why should they care? This is the essence of leadership.

One new organization I was asked to lead had been delivering consistently for some time. They were performing their jobs and functions as they had assumed they always should. But to deliver on the much more challenging road ahead for the organization, they needed something more—something inspirational to drive the team forward. So in a public meeting, I decided to announce that our vision was to become award-winning. This statement shocked people—which was good because it woke them up. It continued to inspire more effort and a different standard of expectation for everyone amongst our peers. It aligned with our purpose and contributed to the vision of a new higher level of excellence, and our immediate mission was therefore clear on how to get there.

What can you do to inspire others, to put a team, or your team, on the path to an exciting new vision? What mission are you on? Inspiring others to align their talents with the Purpose, Vision, and Mission of the organization is what makes for impactful and lasting leadership.

Leadership, Not Titles

Gennady Feller

Gennady Feller is the Founder and President of Safe Partner, a Silicon Valley-based, boutique software development and consulting company serving the world since 1995. A member of the Forbes Business Council and San Francisco Business Times Leadership Trust, Gennady is a full-stack engineer and entrepreneur. His work has improved numerous businesses by handling their software design, development, implementation, ongoing maintenance, and customer support.

Finding Alignment

When I was a kid, I either played with other kids, or I played alone if I didn't like the game the other kids played. As an adult, in most cases, I do the same: I'm either part of a team if I accept what the team does, or I'm building my own team. I don't think this means I was either a natural leader or not. For me, being a leader is just a part of what I'm doing.

I'm not the type to write down a long list of life goals. I focus on doing the things I like and am interested in doing. I'm also interested in learning new things, but it's not an independent goal; it's a part of the overall process. My focus is on achieving what I set out to do. I've never cared about my title.

As for being a leader, I would say that it probably started in middle school. It was in the Soviet Union, so it's hard to find the exact analogy in American terms. I was the class's headman, essentially. It wasn't something I aimed for—in all cases, I was nominated to the position by my classmates. My greatest struggle as a leader has always been with my shyness. I can't say I've fully overcome it. I'm just trying to work with people I'm comfortable with who accept me as I am.

I found that after starting a business, I needed to hire people to help me. Then as the business started to grow, I found myself starting to become a leader. But it wasn't as if I decided to be a leader in advance. I wasn't interested in having some fancy title just for its own sake.

Achievement, Not Meetings

I don't like meetings where people discuss what and how things should be done. If you already know what needs to be done and who can do it, why not just say that and talk about other topics? In rare situations, I will say, "We have to solve this task. I don't know how it should be done. Does anyone know how it should be done?" If a person says that he or she knows, then that person becomes responsible for the task. If no one knows, then we will do what we need to do to try to find an answer.

For cases where I'm assigning a task, no group discussion is needed. In all cases, only one person defines the task and is responsible for seeing that it gets done. This approach has the benefit of reducing the time people spend in meetings. While I'm not opposed to meetings in general, in many cases, they can simply be a waste of time. If you need to assign people responsible for a task, that can be done in other ways.

While I prefer meetings not to run any longer than necessary, this doesn't mean that I don't value feedback or input from others. I allow the team to be a part of any decision. They can openly criticize me, and I often accept this criticism. To function optimally, the team should feel like an organic part of the business process. If the team members like what we are doing, it's very good for motivation. It makes them more focused both on providing valuable feedback and on doing their work as effectively as possible.

Team Dynamics

While I certainly care about team morale, I believe this develops most productively from the work that people do rather than being imposed in a top-down fashion. In other words, instead of calling a meeting to try and convince people they need to unite and collaborate effectively, I prefer to hire people who either have the skill to work well with others or who can develop it. There have certainly been situations where I've hired someone who is good at what they do and knows their stuff but for some reason hasn't worked well with the existing team.

In these situations, it's not reasonable to break up the team we have just to accommodate a new hire, to say, "Listen, we have to work with this person, we have to give them whatever they need and make changes to how we do things." Basically, unless the person is able to change their approach and do what is necessary to contribute constructively, they will not be a good fit for the position and are likely to end up working somewhere else. My experience with new employees is either we can or cannot work together. It's very simple.

This is not to say that I've never worked with people who had a slow start. There's nothing wrong with that. In those cases, for some unexplainable reasons, I believed maybe things just changed with time. And those team members ended up becoming very productive members of the team. It's hard to say exactly why this happens; it may be that for some people you just need to give it time and wait for everything to click into place.

Listening and Learning from Feedback

Leaders must keep two groups foremost in their minds: their customers and their coworkers. In my view, the best strategy to pursue with coworkers is to build a team that is more knowledgeable than you and listen to them and learn from them—to actually gather knowledge and experience from interacting with them.

For example, I might say, "Here is what we're going to do, and it should be done this way." And if the team knows this approach is wrong, they might say to me, "We see what you want to achieve, but there is a better way to do it." That is normal, and I appreciate and respect the skill of the team and their desire to do things the right way. But to just get people together in a meeting and ask them, "What are you thinking?" is, in my view, wasting their time and not the most productive way to get feedback.

By being open to listening to and learning from members of your team, you not only create an environment that stokes creativity by encouraging feedback; you also create a collegial atmosphere that boosts team member loyalty to you and the business.

The Knowledge of a Leader

As a leader, I think knowledge is the most important thing. Knowledge, of course, is important for anyone, but in this case, we're talking about knowledge related to what the person is doing, not knowledge in general. It's true that general knowledge is very important, too. But running a company requires certain specific knowledge; otherwise, you won't know what actions to take or not to take.

In some cases, leaders can be smart people, but perhaps lack some knowledge. To get something specific done, they may need to find other people who have that knowledge. What happens after that? The leader doesn't have enough knowledge to figure out if those people are good or bad—if they really know what they're doing. It means the leader just has to believe them. And maybe the main part of the knowledge required to be a leader in that case is to figure out how good the person you hired or assigned a task to is. Sometimes people will provide a lot of information—graphics, presentations, diagrams—to support the work they are doing, but in reality, it could be done much faster and simpler. But the leader doesn't know that.

This type of approach can work, by the way. There is nothing wrong with it, even if it is not always as efficient as it could be if the leader had more specific knowledge. Because you cannot know everything, at times, you have to hire people who know more than you do about some things. In that case, I wouldn't say to them, "Actually, I don't have the knowledge to figure out if you're on the right track." Instead, just focus on the outcomes and whether or not they can deliver what's needed.

There have been times when I've talked with the team about a task and told them how it should be done, and then a few days later, or whenever it is done, I see the result, and it's been done a different way. In all of these cases, it's been a better solution. While from a business point of view, it's wrong when you set up a task, and it's done in a different way; in my reality, if it works, it works. And it's much better than feedback, because if they had said, when I started the task, "Okay, it should be done differently," we would likely have had a long conversation, and I probably wouldn't understand why it should be different. And I would say, "No, do it my way." But maybe because they know me better than I know myself, they decided, "Okay, let's do this and show him how it should be done." And that works for me.

Customer Relations

I try to listen to the customers because I need to understand them. I need to listen to what they're saying to understand what they want. But in many cases, the customer is not a technical person. The customer, or any person, sees the world in their own way. There are some tasks that need to be solved. But when the customer is trying to explain to me how it should be implemented, and what I should do, rarely can they correctly explain it. Because, again, they're usually not technical people. It's not like the customer says, "I want this," and we're doing something different. Of course not. In most cases, we're doing exactly what the customer wants. The customers are happy. But often—not too often, but often—similar to the example about how the team did a task in a different way than I had originally told them in order to get a good result, we're doing the same thing with customers.

We're trying to solve the customer's problem, not perform the task exactly according to some predefined list. A customer might say, "Okay, I need this, this, and this to improve my business." And we will help them do that. But it doesn't mean, for example, we need to produce what they're asking because they're bored with the functionality or something else. The solution may be different than expected. And so far, it works for me. Because yes, the customer may not be happy at first glance; that's normal. It's not exactly what they asked you to do, and they may say, "Guys, it should be different!" But when they start to use it or look at it, they understand it's exactly what they wanted, or maybe even better.

My goal is to have a mutually beneficial relationship with customers. What I mean is, I'm trying to help customers improve their business. If the customer doesn't really understand how it should be done, that's my mistake, but I'm not spending time trying to convince them, "Okay, customer, it should be done this way. Please allow me." No, I'm just getting the job done.

What Makes a Good Leader?

I think that one indicator of a good leader is when the team still believes in the leader and continues to want to work with them even in the case of failure. It's one thing for a leader to be persistent and persevere in the face of setbacks, but retaining the trust and faith of their team at the same time is essential to overcoming obstacles.

This is why the strongest test of a leader's quality is not how they do when times are good but how they fare when times are tough. If you as a leader can convince your team to keep plugging away and to trust the plan when things appear bleak, you truly deserve to be called a leader.

I don't think that leadership, in and of itself, should be a goal. I believe it's just a part of the process of achieving other goals. People who want to be a leader just for the sake of having a title are not, in my view, likely to make the best leaders.

PART THREE:

MINDSETS

Lessons in the importance of how we think

Leader and Listener

Martin Rowinski

Martin Rowinski is a technology executive with more than twenty-five years of experience providing leadership, developing and implementing strategic processes, and deploying new products to streamline services and improve growth in lead generation and sales. His focus is on the fields of recruiting, finance, technology, marketing, and mortgage lending.

Martin held the role of CTO earlier in his career and is currently the CEO of executive recruitment firm Boardsi, which helps executives connect with companies seeking executive talent that can serve on either a board of directors or board of advisors. The executive recruitment company focuses on specialized services, enabling it to help companies build executive boards and more rapidly and efficiently focus on board diversity to optimize their growth potential and ability to achieve their objectives. Boardsi is a private network for high-level executives who can benefit from its services by finding board positions that match their skill levels.

Martin is also the author of a book called The Corporate Matchmaker, *which can be found on Amazon and at Barnes and Noble. He has been featured on* Forbes Entrepreneur, Fast Company *and* CEO Today. *He writes a monthly article covering leadership for* Forbes Entrepreneur *and* Fast Company.

A Natural Leader

I was born in 1971 and raised in Poland when it was still communist. At that time and place, most people were content to follow and not lead. They were taught to shut up by the system. I was definitely not that guy. I feel like I have always possessed leadership qualities, and even as a kid, I seemed to have the ability to get people to buy in and follow. I don't know why.

Being oppressed did not agree with me even as a young kid. Having the feeling of being told what to do, what to say, or what not to do or say really made no sense to me. I felt like I was not able to express myself and enjoy life to the fullest, and I saw adults who were depressed and struggled daily—this was not my idea of life.

My leadership opportunities died down when I moved to the U.S., mainly due to being picked on because I didn't speak any English. Even though I was shy and a lot quieter through middle school, and even high school, I was still able to make close friends and have a very close bond with a smaller group. This was a group that understood me and knew that, obviously, I was struggling with English. This small group of friends were also mainly immigrants—it was a diverse group of kids, most of whom had an upbringing similar to mine. When I got to college, it all changed, and the old kid Martin came back. I felt that it was easy to jump back into the role of a leader.

My leadership style has definitely changed over time. I had no firm plans in high school, but I believed I was going to do something with my life. Over time, as a new entrepreneur, you encounter some success, and then you hit a wall, or you get knocked down, and you have to get back up. So I adjusted my goals and realized that what I needed to do was set shorter-term objectives to reach the bigger goal. Taking this approach hasn't changed my ultimate goal, which is to be able to help other businesses and also be a mentor to younger people who have an open mind and actually want to listen and absorb information.

Learning to Lead through Struggle

My greatest struggle occurred when I worked for a time with the multilevel marketing company Amway. For this work, you really have to be able to step outside and go shake hands with strangers, introduce yourself to them, show them what you're doing, and talk about your business. When I had my own company, the type of leadership that entailed was easy for me, but this was tough, mainly because it was so different from what I had been doing as a leader, where people looked to me to set the agenda and provide both inspiration and, when needed, hands-on instruction. By contrast, walking up to strangers, shaking their hands, and talking to them required a different approach and, to some degree, a different set of skills.

While that was probably my biggest struggle, at the same time, it was probably the best struggle I put myself through, because it really made me not be "me" and got me out of my comfort zone. Putting yourself outside your comfort zone offers a strong leadership building opportunity. Learning new ways and adjusting your level of comfort prepares you for the unknown. As you can read in many books on leadership, transcending your limitations in this way helps you grow both as a person and as a leader.

Hands-On Leadership and the Dangers of Ego

I would say I am the extreme opposite of a dictator—a leader who uses fear and orders to get results rather than synergy, inspiration, and coaching. I believe in an open-door policy. I am very transparent and honest. I use my personal struggles in life and, as an example, would never ask anybody to do something that I can't do myself. Literally, I'll get my hands dirty, if that's what it takes to show somebody how to do something the right way. I would say I'm a hands-on leader.

I've always joked that my leadership ability was more of an impatience thing, where I can either talk to somebody, or I can say, "Get out of the way! Let me show you how it's done." But that was just naïve, young me. I have evolved over time as a leader, and my patience has grown significantly. I'm no longer short-fused like I used to be.

One of the most important lessons in leadership I learned was when I was a consultant for a company, and the CEO there was the extreme opposite of what any leader should be. I've never seen anybody with such a huge ego. I tried to help him, but his ego was just too big to allow him to take advice from anyone else. As a leader, you can never think you know everything and you can no longer learn from anyone. Good leaders are never done learning; they should never feel like they know everything. Learn to take advice. Never stop learning!

I've worked with other leaders who were comfortable with coming to me and asking me for advice. They would take the advice and actually use it versus this guy who would sit there and waste my time for eight hours and then not take any of my advice. What I got out of that was, don't waste your time attempting to help somebody who has an ego that big. Some people are just impossible to help; you have to want to be helped to get help.

Individualizing Motivation

I found over time that some people truly believe that money is the ultimate motivator. I don't believe that myself. Yes, money is definitely a helpful thing for people when they're struggling, or something comes up. But as far as the day-to-day, Monday-through-Friday work environment, it's not the only motivator. Money should be a means to an end, not an end in itself. The point is to create purpose with our money, not make our driving factor achieving money for its own sake. It's what we do with it that matters. Many people their quit jobs, and they even go out and get a job that's paying them less money in order to find something that they are happy with.

I try to individualize motivating each team and each individual. I wouldn't say I have a specific way to motivate people; it's literally different for everybody. I try to learn everybody's personality, and I adapt to it. If I see that they're struggling with a certain job task, I try to figure it out and sometimes find that's not even the job that they should be doing. Maybe their talent lies somewhere else. I find that when people love their job, they become motivated themselves—enthusiasm for what people are doing naturally creates joy in their work.

Going back to the example that excessive ego should never be part of a leader, I'm perfectly prepared to say I'm an imperfect leader. I make mistakes on a daily basis, and I think, as a leader, it's good if you can admit your mistakes, whether it's to your partners or your employees.

People also respect a hands-on approach. Of course, you get to a certain point in a company where hands-on just doesn't work. But I think—especially when you're an entrepreneur, and you're growing in the beginning—if somebody knows that the CEO literally has done every job in the company, it gets a lot of respect.

I also think group meetings are awesome motivational tools. While I prefer offsite locations, onsite can work as well.

The Qualities of a Leader

One way to learn what it takes to be a good leader is to read the top authors on the subject. Going through high school and college, I always struggled with reading, because you're forced to read. I came out of college thinking, "I'm never picking up a book." And then somebody told me I would love reading Og Mandino. I picked up a book by him, and they were absolutely right. He uses storytelling in a very motivational way that is easy to read. Napoleon Hill is also a great author and storyteller, along with Dale Carnegie. *As a Man Thinketh* by James Allen is a very short book that uses simple language to show how powerful our thoughts can be in guiding our lives in a positive direction.[9] I also think the Bible is super motivational, and I read it on a daily basis.

I love saying, "God gave me two ears and one mouth for a reason." As a leader, you should listen a lot more than you talk. For me, being able to listen is probably the number one quality for a leader; don't talk over people, and always end a sentence with a question. So even if somebody asks

---

[9] James Allen, As a Man Thinketh, 1903.

you a question, you can answer it, and then you can ask them a question back, creating a conversation that can really get people to open up and talk more.

Skill-wise, especially these days, always stay on top of tech. If you want to be a good leader, be aware of what technology is out there, at least to the point of understanding it well enough that you can discuss it intelligently. With technology increasingly becoming a major competitive advantage, knowing the latest tech trends helps you determine how to use them effectively in your business.

Some people will tell you success for a leader is purely financial. So if your goal is to make a million dollars, and you've done that—great, you're successful. For me, though, it's definitely not just financial. That is part of it, obviously. But the goal, in my view, should not be making money for money's sake. For instance, money comes and goes, but family is forever. As a result, cultivate values that place family first and view money as a tool in its service. I believe successfully finding the balance between family life, friend life, and business life is vital—meaning, you don't want your kids to say, "I don't want to talk to my dad or my mom ever again." Or if you can't communicate with your spouse, then you're failing as a leader. Be a spiritual leader as well. Don't just advise people—inspire them.

I ultimately think if you focus on nonfinancial intangibles like relationships and connecting with others, the financial things just come naturally. They might not come as quickly as you want, but they do eventually come. For me, for example, because I was so focused on family, when I went through a divorce and lived as a single dad, my kids always took priority, even though I was an entrepreneur. I coached soccer, which requires a significant time commitment that, obviously, slowed down my entrepreneurship. But I knew one day they were going to grow up and become adults. And they did. So success just came a little bit late, but that's okay.

The Mindset of a Leader

I am sure there are things in there that I would have done differently. It's like the old saying, "If I could be a twenty-five-year-old with the fifty-one-year-old me right now, would I do things differently?" One hundred percent, I would. My confidence level would be different. But for the things that I did do, I wouldn't do anything differently. Even the struggles and the hard times, I wouldn't change them because those are the things that are responsible for who I am today.

I would say, step up to the edge and dive. Don't hesitate. Don't be scared. Just go for it. You're going to make mistakes. Keep an open mind, don't have an inflated ego, and surround yourself with a mastermind group or at least advisors or mentors. I didn't have mentors, but I found mentorship in books. So if you don't have mentors, pick up the books and read them. I often say if the Henry Fords, the Dale Carnegies, and the Napoleon Hills were alive today, everybody would want to be their friend and have them as a mentor, but the great thing is they wrote everything down in a book—the answers are there. So just pick up the book and mentor yourself by having a conversation with them through the book. That would be my advice.

As a leader, you will fail—don't be afraid to fail. Just get out there. What doesn't kill you makes you stronger. Genuinely listening to others fosters real and lasting connections and drives motivation. And what motivates your success helps you motivate others to succeed.

Live Another Day

M. Nicolette Freeman, M.S, M.B.A.

Nicolette Freeman is a senior executive, IT strategist, and transformational leader, recognized as a transformation expert and influential C-Suite partner. She currently serves as Vice President and Senior Partner with IBM Consulting where she heads North America Global Business Services. A champion for customer centricity, Nicolette deploys advanced analytical methodologies to identify opportunities, reengineer processes and technology, and optimize operational excellence.

Before joining the corporate sector, Nicolette was a U.S. Air Force Officer. She served on several global tours, including Iraq and Kuwait. In her last role as Logistics and Programs Director for Air Force Space Command, she managed a $42B global outsourced avionics contract and was recognized for outstanding Airforce Leadership by the U.S. Inspector General. Her previous command positions included Director of Logistics Support Division for the U.S. Air Force Academy; Joint Basing Director/Strategic Initiatives in Washington, DC; Logistics Readiness Squadron Commander; and Director of Operations in Iraq and Kuwait.

Nicolette can be reached at https://speakerhub.com/speaker/icolette-freeman.

Every Life Is Worth Living

It's a fact. The very breath that you breathe was created for you, for this moment in time. Inhale it deeply. Take in each crisp note of beauty, energy, and promise. Life begins and ends with one single breath. It is the breaths in between that matter. Those long, deep breaths. You inhale to energize, recharge, renew, restore, acclimate, and accelerate your life's every desire. Inhale it now, this very breath. It is your starting line. As you train for the race that lies ahead, commit yourself to exhale old thought patterns, regrets, delays, and distractions. That is the key ingredient to leadership, to live in the now. Design your life with an adjustable blueprint and turn your tragedies into triumphs!

Join me through this journey, and live the life designed for you. Inhale the fresh air of new promises and imaginations, new outcomes and endeavors. Take a moment, recognize it as one of the most significant moments of your life, and embrace your very own design for life.

The Triathlon

The design for my life has undergone considerable evolution throughout my career. It is best summarized with my morning mantra "Seize the moment and live another day!" I describe my career journey as a triathlon. It is filled with endurance, rapid transitions, anticipation, disappointments, and expectation to win championships. Visualize how races begin: hearts racing, participants energized, crowds cheering, everyone waiting for the opening gunshot, that universal signal that the race has begun. In an instant, competitors transform potential energy into a kinetic firestorm. Yes, races are exhilarating, fulfilling, and at times, they are draining. They begin with a quick burst of action and the stamina that is required to compete at peak performance. Within each of our lives, there are races that we must run and win to achieve our goals. There are also many races where we run alongside others. Great leaders recognize this difference and know how to set the pace for both. These are the races that foundationally shape who we are and who we become.

In the first leg of my triathlon, I was a United States Air Force officer. After years of training, I was eager to begin serving our nation at McGuire AFB in New Jersey. At that same point early in my career, I started a family. During this first tour, I began to understand how important it is to master self-regulation and emotional intelligence. I reported to active duty three months before the attacks of September 11. As I juggled the responsibilities of a new officer, new wife, and new mother, my duty station became the primary operation for FEMA rescue and recovery. All at once, the cataclysmic events of 9/11 sucked the air out of our nation, and the race we were running abruptly stopped. There was no time for handoffs or recovery stretches. It was war! So what do you do when the blueprints designed for your life abruptly become obsolete? What is your recovery plan when you reach the end of your blueprint and must rely on newly adjusted realities?

Simply put, the answer is emotional intelligence, the superpower of legendary leadership. Without it, leaders are ill-equipped to run their leg of the race or process the myriad of mental demands of daily life. Human beings encounter over four hundred emotional experiences every single day. Each can become a daunting task that requires energy, resilience, and emotional discipline. Positive emotional encounters shape how we relate to one another and humanity, and positive experiences create moments that matter. They release energy that uplifts and encourages. Negative encounters can leave us fumbling through the dark. We gasp for air, doubt our life purpose, and might miss key opportunities to turn tragedies into triumphant outcomes.

What 9/11 taught us is that fatalities are final, but not all finalities are fatal. If you have the breath of life, all possibilities still exist. Those known and unknown possibilities are yours for the taking. They are living proof that your dreams, ambitions, and life designs are all works in progress. When we accept those possibilities, we are armed with hope and strength to encourage and uplift our teams and families. My air force career was filled with plans, designs, places, and roles that I never dreamt possible. The most rewarding part was to know that through it all, service members were dedicated to our nation's and humanity's greater good. However, even the most amazing careers with the most incredible colleagues end.

Finality: The Mission to Transition

My transition into corporate America was a design like no other. It was like swimming and cycling at the same time. This transition can be chaotic and unharmonious. It requires self-reflection, discovery, composure, new resources, and the ability to see opportunities. Most service members begin this portion of the race ill-equipped for the leadership challenges that manifest when they struggle to find their footing on new terrain. Let's call it a race with an extraordinarily long recovery time. No matter how long you have trained for it, you are never ready for the finality of the finish line. You lose a part of your identity. You hear your first name for the rest of your life!

As I transitioned into corporate America, I was privileged to build countless high-performance teams. The team that I will never forget had fantastic synergy. Each member possessed a superpower that words cannot describe. I will never forget my last hire, Mike. Mike and I met at a military hiring expo, and this man was larger than life! He illuminated the entire edifice—every crevice. I knew that I had to meet him. Have you ever met a leader like that? Someone whose electricity can light up Wall Street, a visionary who makes the world a better place through their presence, philanthropy, and commitment to the greater good—a person who runs their race and comes back for the rest of us. That was Mike. Seven seconds with him and you felt empowered to solve the most complex, audacious problems in the universe. I hired Mike because I knew he would not only transform corporate America but me as well—I knew I would learn from him in the process. He accomplished both through his life and death.

I wasn't sure if it was the finality of it or how helpless I felt when I received the text. Mike shot himself! I fell to my knees, immobilized and speechless. Wait…what? I quickly texted his wife and simultaneously called her. After she answered, there was a long pause. Everything I had hoped for was instantly extinguished. We lost a man who was larger than life.

In an instant, an air force pilot, executive, White House Fellow, Congressional Liaison, husband, father, minister, marathoner, triathlete, son, brother, and friend left this earth in a devastating event that permanently changed the blueprints of thousands of lives. I pray you never see that day! Singular events in our lives can leave the strongest warrior and the greatest leaders utterly immobilized, and this was mine. Mike's death was never considered in the plans and projects I had for him or part of the original design for his life. It was an irreversible event that forced many humans to come to terms with mortality. Mike wasn't just my employee. No, he was a high-performance team all by himself! Utterly brilliant, remarkably astute, a visionary and luminary, he created a lifelong impact through every life he touched.

The greatest struggle that leaders encounter is to know what to do when humanity's fatal flaws knock on our doors or appear in our reflections! These are moments that matter for a lifetime. They are opportunities that present decisions and actions.

Recover or Succumb

Leading high-performance teams through irreversible tragedy is one of our most difficult life challenges. Some decisions cannot be reversed. Yet legendary leaders place their anchors deep in the sea. When the storms of life rage and torrential downpours come, they are securely anchored and thrive in any circumstance, including irreversible ones. As I examine my career and review the fatal flaws in my own reflection, I am reminded of three critical truths. First, a short memory is the key to forward momentum. Mistakes you make cannot and should not define you. You must love yourself enough to cast your flaws in the sea of forgetfulness and live another day. Second, discovering who you are is a purposeful element within your design for life. Legendary leaders know who and whose they are. They have deep roots and lifelines that cultivate purpose and power in their lives. And third, fatal flaws aren't final. Edward J. Stieglitz, M.D. said it best:

"The important thing to you is **not how many years in your life, but how much life in your years!"**

Lessons from a Vine

After losing Mike and stabilizing my team, I discovered that few places provide me with the type of mental clarity, agility, and restoration that I found on the island of Santorini, Greece. An oasis of riveting sunsets and incredible blue waters, the island is home to the unique Assyrtiko vine, grown in cliff-side "terroir" conditions, a combination of soil composition, harsh weather, and topography. The vine is an iconic symbol of enduring leadership and self-renewal, pulling minerals and energy from the soil into its fruit.

For four thousand years, people in Greece have made wine, and Santorini's vineyards are believed to be some of the oldest in continuous production. Considered to be some of the oldest vines on the planet, they grow on the epicenter of one of the most violent volcanic eruptions in earth's history, where they have managed to survive and thrive. This terroir is any other plant's hell. Strong, constant winds sweep from all directions, rainfall is rare, and the soil is too porous to retain scarce water. Despite those obstacles, common wisdom is that stressed vines produce better wines, and Santorini vineyards produce the finest wine that money can buy. For centuries, Assyrtiko vines have been trained into shapes that resemble baskets, so strong winds cannot damage new growth. The vineyards thrive even when vinedressers are exhausted and the climb to them seems impossible.

They are the only European grape that is resistant to the most destructive insect pest known to grapes, drawing their resistance from the volcanic ash in which they grow. It is an adaptive, resilient, opportunistic, unflappable, enduring, and brilliantly indestructible survivor!

Deep roots of these vines grown in the harsh terroir provide lifelines amidst their volatile ecosystem. The vine transforms potential energy stored in its deep roots into kinetic outcomes every moment, producing wines that connect modern wine culture to Greece's ancient past. Coveted for its full body, the Assyrtiko adapts well when planted in other regions and countries. It accomplishes its purpose at the hands of vinedressers who prune, cultivate, and crush its precious fruit. In many ways, this vine is my story: an exhausting journey through volatile ecosystems with vinedressers who collectively nourished my soul, shaped my character, and enriched my career.

Until now, it is likely that you never considered the process of curating one of the finest wines in the world or the parallels between exceptional wine and unforgettable leaders. They both begin with deep roots. They withstand explosive circumstances. They adapt to survive. They self-renew.

Changing Lives Forever

Alexis Zen

For over twenty years, Alexis Zen has been working in top Fortune 500 companies all around the world, focusing on change, transformation, and process improvements. Having a passion for self-development and a calling to help people achieve their dreams has led him to create a powerful step-by-step process that will transform your life forever.

When Alexis built the wellness company Mindbodism, developed a mobile app for it, wrote a self-help book, lost 7 kilos, and launched the basketball platform Basketble in just three months, while working full time in a bank and had to care for his newborn baby, he realized that time is an illusion, and anyone can achieve what they want.

He now shares his knowledge and experience through his life coaching, his books, and the online course "The Power of 1 Second: How to achieve anything you want," enabling others to become healthier, happier, and more successful.

Alexis is also a motivational speaker, writer, entrepreneur, and teacher of Meditation, Qi Gong, Yoga, Kundalini Awakening and Latin dance. He is a Life Coach, Level 3 Reiki, and Transcendental Meditation (TM) Practitioner.

He loves helping change people's lives and bringing their dreams to fruition. You can connect with Alexis at: www.alexiszen.com, www.mindbodism.com, or www.basketble.com.

The Power of 1 Second

In the beginning, there was no goal. It was just a feeling; an inner calling that could not be resisted. It started four years ago when a voice in my head told me I need to write a book about "The Power of 1 Second." It was nothing more than a simple idea that was stacked in my head. I wrote one page in the first year, and I always knew I would eventually write the book. However, it was not until last year that in one second, something changed inside me, and I started writing nonstop for three months. The first draft was complete, and then again in one second, I realized that some very powerful transformation had happened to be able to finish it in three months. In order to write the book, *The Power of 1 Second: How to Achieve Anything You Want*, I did extensive research on all the best self-help books and articles on neuroscience, Indian, and Chinese practices and used my own inner guidance.[10]

Then I had another calling, which told me to help people. The voice told me that if in three months I was able to write the book, *The Power of 1 Second*, lose seven kilograms, improve my relationship with my wife, care for my newborn son, build an online platform for one of my businesses—basketble.com, where I help people find a place to play basketball—then I need to share this knowledge with the rest of the world. There is nothing more fulfilling than helping people and sharing the knowledge and experience you have with them, then seeing them transform their lives and create a better world.

[10] Alexis Zen, The Power of 1 Second: How to Achieve Anything You Want, 2022.

Then, again in one second, I had another calling to create a new business which I called Mindbodism. Mindbodism is committed to helping people train their bodies, rewire their minds, and awaken their spirits to become healthier, happier, and more successful. I realised that the main reason for my success and ability to be able to perform at much higher levels in three months and complete activities that I was trying to complete in four years was because I was able to exercise and balance my mind, body, and spirit. As of the time of this writing, it is still at a very early stage, where I am developing the products, but people can visit www.mindbodism.com and find practices, meditations, Qi Gong, High Intensive Training Workouts, as well as reading or listening to book summaries, learning different breathing techniques to reduce stress and anxiety, and much more.

In the beginning, it was an inner calling to write the book *The Power of 1 Second*. Now, it is my life purpose to build mindbodism.com and help improve the lives of millions of people.

Short-Term Goals Make a Map to Your Long-Term Destination

There are many ways to achieve something in your life. Some people will start by having only short-term goals. Others will start with long-term goals, and still, others will not have any goals. There is no right or wrong way of doing things, and as explained in my book, your life can significantly change in one second, and you will never know in the moment if the decision you make now is right or wrong. However, by having long-term goals and breaking them down into short-term goals, you can achieve things faster because you will not only be more focused but also have a direction to know where you are going.

It is like wanting to go from point A to point B without a map. You can still reach point B without a map by driving to many places until you find point B, or you can determine where you want to go and complete short-term goals to help you reach point B faster. So if my long-term goal was to visit a city, I could create shorter goals like how much gas I will need, how much money I will need, which route I need to take to reach my destination, etc.

Also—especially if the goal is big and complex—you will need to create a plan and a map which will show how your shorter goals will help you achieve your long-term goals, which goals are the dependencies, and which are the priorities that you need to follow to make sure you can achieve your long-term goals at the specified time.

The beginning of my journey was to write the book *The Power of 1 Second*, but there was a time that in one second, I realised that this book and the course I was going to create based on it were just a small part of what I wanted to do. I wanted to help people become healthier, happier, and more successful by training their bodies, rewiring their brains, and awakening their spirits. This moment did not come after extensive thinking. It came naturally during one of my meditations, and I just knew I had to do it. Once you have clarity of an idea, then you need to analyse it and test it. I knew from experience that people who do not like reading books will be interested in trying new experiences, workouts, and practices. Then I discussed these ideas with my friends and tested a few practices and meditations, which were very appealing—and then I realised I had to focus my effort on a bigger purpose and create and develop mindbodism.com.

The pivot from writing a book to creating a new health and wellness business was not easy. It required a lot more effort and a lot more money. As it has a holistic approach and exercises mind, body, and spirit, I had to study a lot to get qualifications and partner with other experts to be able to deliver my products. However, when you start small, do not give up, and if you continue and persist, you will find a way to achieve anything you want. It was a big challenge to start a new business while I already had basketble.com. I was working full time in one of the banks in London, and I had a newborn baby that needed my support, since my wife was in bed due to health issues. But you need to start small, and even though I am not fully there yet, my heart is telling me that I am doing the right thing, because this business is going to benefit a lot of people. And when you know that you are not driven by your ego or your "self," but motivated by the good of mankind, you know it will be successful and is the right thing to do. And that is exactly what happened to me.

Pivot Toward Success

A few months after creating mindbodism.com, I was informed by the bank I worked for that my role was moving to a different city outside London, and I would have to relocate, even though I was working for them for eight years. I was terrified. I had an eighteen-month-old son. I just had a newborn daughter, got a new mortgage, and my grandmother just passed away. I could relocate to the other city and keep my job and live in a city I do not like or change my life forever. Before completing the practices from Mindbodism, a challenge like this would cause me fear, anxiety, and stress. However, now I only see magic and meaning in everything that happens in my life.

The magic started two years ago when I said I will publish *The Power of 1 Second: How to Achieve Anything You Want* in November 2022 and that it will become a bestseller. Since then, every morning when I wake up, I visualise my book becoming a bestseller and repeat that I will publish it in November 2022. This is the exact month that my contract will end with the bank I was working for. By not accepting the relocation, I would get three months of displacement, which will help me make my dream come true and make *The Power of 1 Second* a bestseller. Is the date a coincidence, or did I change my future by changing my thoughts and manifesting what I really wanted?

When you are connected with your true self, the universe will bring you what you ask for, and you will find meaning and purpose in whatever you do. Also, remember this:

> "Sometimes the bad things that happen in our lives put us directly on the path to the best things that will ever happen to us. So have faith."

My nature has always been to help people, and this is where I help everyone for free (until my money runs out). Also, it seems when you offer your services for free, the universe will also give you things for free, as only last week, I was selected by Mckinsey Consulting to attend a four-week-long leadership training for free. Help others and others will help you.

Luckily, I was able to see results immediately before even creating a product. When I discussed my business with friends and family, they were very keen to help me, and they began to book sessions with me to help them train their bodies, rewire their minds, and awaken their spirits. A lot of people only focus on one area, and they can be great, but when you balance your body, mind, and spirit, you will be able to experience something new. You will be able to see connections and purpose in whatever you do, but most importantly, you will realise that everyone is connected, and we are all ONE. This is the reason I am planning to publish my second book called *My Spiritual Reality* in November 2023, where I will explain what you will experience when you are awakened and when you reach Oneness, which is what happened to me.

Another important aspect of pivoting from writing a book to building a new business is that it changed the way I measure success. Before, I was only focusing on sales, profitability, and numbers, and even though these are important, they should not be your main focus. Your focus should be to help people and create value for them so they can be happier, healthier, and more successful. In that way, you will be successful in whatever you do because money after a certain point is not important. None of the great leaders were motivated by money but rather by following a cause that they believed in, a cause that was worth dying for.

There were many moments in my life when I thought I was stuck, and I could not pivot or persist in my cause. However, using the concepts from my book *The Power of 1 Second*, I was always able to find new ways of doing things, overcoming obstacles and challenges, and having clarity of mind on what I needed to do next. Concepts in the book are powerful because you will realize that it only takes one second to start an action that will move you closer to your goal. Also, by following the learning process described, you will be able to achieve what you want without making sacrifices.

Many times, people ask me the question, "Alexis, when should I pivot, and when should I persist in the path that I am following?" and my answer is always the same: "Once you balance mind, body, and spirit, you will know because you will connect with your inner self and know what you need to do next, as you will have clarity of mind." Even if the decision you take leads you to unwanted results, maybe you need to learn from your mistakes to reach the next level. However, do not let a failure stop you from doing what your gut tells you to do. Speak with experts in the field before you pull the plug or try something else, because a lot of times, you will not see immediate results, but the results will come if you continue.

Therefore, if you love and believe in what you are doing, you need to persist. However, if it does not work, you need to try different approaches, different products, different customers, and different propositions and speak with experts in the field to understand what is working and what is not working. Once you complete this type of analysis, you will be able to make a better decision as to whether you need to pivot or persist.

Move Like Water

A successful venture is one that lasts for many years. But how can a business last when the only constant thing is change? The answer is "Move like water." Water is always able to find a path because it adapts and changes shape every time it finds an obstacle. What I am doing to make my businesses last is to build a strong foundation with great people, have consistent processes, and develop products that will not only add value to people's lives but also change their lives forever.

Understanding People Will Clear a Path for Success

Chris Roberts

Chris Roberts is the founder and CEO of Sterling Rhino Capital, LLC. He has been an entrepreneur and real estate investor since 2007. Chris specializes in investor relations, commercial debt, and managing financials.

He began his real estate ventures by renovating, flipping, building, and renting single-family residences before moving on to larger properties. In addition to running his own property management company to manage his smaller properties, Chris focuses his efforts on helping others create passive cash flow by investing in large, 100+ plus unit multifamily apartment buildings. He has led Sterling Rhino to acquire and manage 1,122 units across the country with an estimated value of more than $122 million.

Chris is an author and member of the Forbes Real Estate Council. He has been a contributor on BiggerPockets *and also hosts the* Charging Forward *podcast where he interviews extraordinary entrepreneurs. He is an enterprise partner with Feeding America and is passionate about teaching and giving back to the community. Chris enjoys spending time with his wife, Christina, and traveling the world. He and Christina have been married for eleven years and have two dogs, Bentley and Oliver.*

Leadership Qualities

At fifteen, I was responsible for my own life. My path to leadership at this young age was a strong work ethic and a positive attitude. Not having a formal education, I had to outwork those around me to shine professionally. Around the age of eighteen, I came across a mentor who changed my life for the better. He demonstrated what leadership was all about, enlightening me on the importance of reading, which I used to refine my leadership skills. I didn't realize it yet, but that mentor had put me on the right path to success.

At the time, I didn't exactly have a vision beyond the end of the week. I focused on surviving, proving my worth to my peers, and figuring out how to make it. Without a positive circle of influence guiding me, my goals were simply to make it from A to B. I had no delusions of grandeur. If anything, I was selling myself short. Once I met my mentor, I started developing life skills and writing down goals. Now the sky's the limit. It wasn't always that way. The minute I had a vision of what I wanted out of life was when I discovered the mindset of creating goals.

Finding the Leader Within

A formal education provides you with more than just knowledge. It makes you feel like you belong. It gives you the confidence to use your skills. I struggled to convince myself that my skills were worthy of managing others. Not just getting the title of manager and the pay raise that goes with it, but actually leading people. How did I overcome my fear? I worked my tail off. I made mistakes. But I was fortunate enough to have my mentor pull me aside to say,

"Hey, that's ok. That's actually part of the process. Don't fear mistakes."

I learned that's actually how you become a great leader: stumbling and learning from those setbacks. I overcame my fear by making mistakes and taking lessons from every single one. Without realizing it, I led by example. I was enthusiastic about the work I was doing. I've since learned people actually gravitate towards leaders who exude positive energy. I didn't consider it a skill. It was just who I was. Fortunately, mentors and supervisors came into my life and built business skills around my positive attitude. That's how I evolved into a great leader.

I took my energy, my enthusiasm, my work ethic, and my attitude and combined them with educating myself on how the business worked, from reading spreadsheets to reading colleagues. I led by doing. As I've matured, though, I've realized leadership is more about demonstrating and articulating than simply knowing what to do. I show people how to do it, explain to them why, and let them know how it's effective. My skills evolved from personality traits to acquired skills. When you combine those two, I believe you've found the recipe for success.

Vision of Leadership

My vision of leadership changed completely when I met my mentor. When I grew up, I never imagined more than a paycheck-to-paycheck existence. That's how I defined "success." The good life was simple. Beyond that, "rich people" flew on private jets, drove fancy cars, and lived in massive houses. That felt so far out of my reach that I didn't even dare dream to achieve so much. That's when I met the first individual who lived a life like the one that felt so out of reach to me. A life with complete financial freedom. He didn't act like a stereotypical "rich" man, yet he was tremendously successful. He retired at the age of forty-four and started a family fun center because he loves kids. He owned real estate and had several rental properties. Finally, I saw a wealthy guy I could relate to. He looked like me, worked like me, and had the same positive attitude in his day-to-day. I didn't think financial success was for people like us. He proved otherwise.

For the first time in my life, I realized not all successful people flaunt their wealth. Often, the wealthiest are the ones you never suspect are wealthy and successful. They just go about their lives, inspiring people, demonstrating excellent leadership through their hard work. These folks are good at teaching others. Meeting this person instilled an early foundation of giving back and teaching. I realized an average person like me could actually make a difference in the world. That dramatically changed the way I see the world, especially what it means to be wealthy and successful. And more importantly, what I would need to attain both.

Motivating Others, Motivating Self

Whoever stands before you, be it your coworkers or your own reflection, motivation starts with the right attitude. Obstacles pop up no matter how well you plan around them. When my team comes to me with negativity, I reframe the conversation: "Hey, let's hold on for a second. Tell me something positive that happened today. Tell me something good that could arise from this circumstance. Let's talk about how we could turn the problem into a solution."

Attitude influences our reaction to the problem. The wrong attitude drags us down. When we start with a negative outlook, it's difficult to see the problem clearly enough to solve it. That's why I start my team on a positive note every day, approaching problems as challenges we just haven't overcome yet. A problem is another word for "opportunity." Put in the work and solve it.

Sometimes at work, situations arise that aren't part of my job description but are essential to the success of our company. I'm not afraid to confront a new problem because I want to learn and I want my team to see that any of us are capable of overcoming unforeseen problems. Most importantly, a problem may require more than one person to solve. Perhaps, if we all work together, we can fix it. If I'm working through the problem with the team, and we arrive at the solution together, it inspires them. They'll say, "I'm shocked at how early Chris is up. I'm shocked at how he answers text messages late at night and how he works on the weekends. I mean, the guy just never stops." I wear that like a badge of honor because I want my team to see that the team leader puts in the most work instead of taking credit for theirs.

Adapting Is "The Art of War"

I read *The Art of War* by Sun Tzu when I began my entrepreneurial journey.[11] Not only did I find the strategies in this book helped me adapt to the changing nature of business, but that also many other business owners I encountered utilized the same strategies, solidifying the book's value in my eyes.

---

[11] Sun Tzu, The Art of War (Lionel Giles, 1910).

The basic premise is to always plan and anticipate the competition that can affect your business. You must plan, in good and bad times, to stay ahead of anything that can derail your business. If you are having an amazing year, then set up systems to protect you for when business is bad. If you are in the middle of a recession then tighten up, get efficient, and outmaneuver the competition to earn more market share, ensuring your survival. Constant change is a certainty in business. The question is, will you and your team embrace the change and thrive? Or fade away from existence because you failed to anticipate change?

Values of a Leader

What a leader values depends upon the size of the team they're leading. If you lead a gigantic corporation, your value proposition may have changed from when you started at the company. I can tell you that our business is run with ethics, integrity, and people in mind. We are not solely focused on money and growth because we know those qualities will come if we do the right thing.

Knowing what "the right thing" is can be difficult in business. Sometimes you lose profits by doing the right thing. It can be hard to have difficult conversations. Many avoid tough conversations so they don't need to deal with the adversity of getting on the same page. Not living up to your values will come back to haunt you as a leader.

Our value proposition has always been to take care of each other and take care of our investors. With that mindset, things tend to work out. What does it mean to put people first?

If we don't know each other, and we're discussing an investment opportunity, I have to treat you like a family member because I need you to trust that I will do the right thing with your money. You may ask me a lot of personal questions to feel comfortable with my advice. I have to be a real human being when I work with you. I can't rush you off the phone because I have another call in five minutes. If I do have to jump off the call, I will call you back right away so that you feel like you are literally the most important client I have.

This is because the person in the room is always the most important person to us. It can be challenging to sustain these values as your business scales up. Growth can dilute a leader's values. The more people come into a company, the more important it is to reiterate your values with everyone. Never forget where your values came from. Never forget why you built this company. Never become so focused on profit that you lose sight of what your true values are.

A leader must be able to look in the mirror and answer honestly. As you rise to the top, it's easy to step back and allow your coworkers to take on all the work. The problem is that you become complacent. You lose touch with what it meant to chip rocks in the beginning. You have been riding on the express train so long that you forget how it felt to spend eighty hours a week building the railroad.

A leader needs to keep an eye on the basics, or they risk losing touch with the team they lead.

Three Aspects of Leadership

Leadership is a constant process of evolution and self-education. If you're not growing, you're declining. A leader has to juggle three aspects of his or her personal life in order to effectively lead others:

1. Financial Health. We have to take care of our personal finances if we are to be responsible for the finances of others.
2. Physical and Mental Fitness. We have to take care of our bodies and minds.
3. Family and Friends. We have to be sure the people we care about are well.

Managing these three aspects of your life will make you a better leader. If you're not dedicated to these elements in your personal life, you can't provide the diligent service your clients deserve.

Identify Your Weaknesses to Find Strength in Others

The greatest asset a leader can possess is the ability to measure strengths and weaknesses, both in themselves and others. The best way to address a personal weakness is to hire people who excel in that area, people you can trust. For example, if your people skills are strong, and you lead by example, but struggle with slowing down and implementing processes to help your company grow to the next level, hire a COO or president to take those tasks off your plate.

Know where you need help, identify people who can provide that help, then utilize their strengths as a bulwark against your own perceived weakness. This requires something that CEOs have in short supply: humility. The number one quality of good leadership is surrounding yourself with people you can treat as equals. Make people feel like they're working with you instead of working for you. A leader's greatest asset is identifying the skills of the people surrounding them.

Measuring Success vs. Failure

I measure success by the lives that we touch around us. I've been fortunate to have a lot of success, mostly through hard work. Once you get past the first few levels of success, you see the impact your work has on others. For instance, recently my work with Feeding America fed a million people. That effort changed lives for the better. Success is mentoring people through your business model and using your professional experience to help refine their own. It's seeing the smiling faces of clients experiencing the power of watching their money go to work for them.

What excites me most about leadership is the influence we share with the world. We have the power to improve people's lives. All business owners have that power.

Leaders also fail. While traditionally, failure is seen as a negative, I've found there are many lessons to be learned from it. Yes, it stings to fail. But ultimately, failure teaches you what doesn't work. You may lose something: money, friends, clients. At the end of the day, if they don't ride out failure with you, they probably weren't on board to begin with. If you keep pushing ahead and working hard, you'll make it back. And those who stick with you will forget that failure as you continue to succeed.

Advice to Anyone Starting Out

If I woke up tomorrow and had to start my career all over, I would change a few things.

Number one, I would have started reading aggressively much earlier. That would have inspired me to take more chances early on, too. Building a successful sales and marketing career took a while. I didn't start reading financial books and real estate guides until my mid-thirties. That delayed when I started investing and taking chances, like buying real estate.

Number two, I wish I would have purchased real estate earlier. I missed out on early opportunities and continue to regret it. Real estate is a powerful business. I wish I had put my ego away, listened more, and bought some property early on.

My advice to anyone starting out on their leadership journey is to have humility and appreciate those around you. A good leader understands the job and experiences of all employees, at every level. If you can understand the perspective of others when you're leading, you can lead in a constructive way.

Be humble, work hard, and value others.

Lead With Love, Not Fear

A'sha Love

A'sha Love is the founder of Multidimensional U®, a multidimensional, multimedia company specializing in the expansion of human consciousness. Through her online metaphysical programs and events, she has helped people over the world contribute to a New Earth through the alchemy of their personal transformation. In addition, she's helped them uncover their soul calling and activate incredible innate physical abilities. Since 2015, A'sha has led experiential programs for people awakening to a greater multidimensional reality.

After getting her undergraduate degree from William Smith College and her MA from Michigan Tech University, A'sha founded several nonprofit organizations and launched a consulting business before her metaphysical awakening catapulted her into alignment with her own greater calling.

Her warm, loving approach provides a high-vibrational, nurturing container that helps people shift out of destructive patterns that stem from core wounding and the trauma of living in lower-density and negative programming. Many of A'sha's clients have become powerful, impactful healers and Wayshowers in their own right. A'sha has been featured as an expert in the areas of Multidimensional Physics, Personal Transformation, and the Multidimensional Self.

Her work has appeared on channels like Higher Self and Higher Self Portal. A'sha spends time with her family between the Appalachian Mountains of North Carolina, her beloved Finisterre (France), and the many different dimensions of the multiverse. She can be contacted at info@multidimensionalu.com.

Discovering the Leader Within

There is a story that my mother used to tell about a time when I was just three years old. My younger neighborhood friend and I were missing one rainy afternoon. My mother began to grow worried. Just as she was about to go looking for us, there I was on the horizon, coming down the street in my rain boots, holding my little friend's hand. Apparently, I was just as confident as could be, bringing us both safely back home. The way my mother tells it, she was struck by the otherworldliness of a toddler behaving in that way. I seemed fearless. For me, it has always felt natural to guide others back home.

When I grew a bit older, my inborn impulse to help others gain greater freedom manifested itself in activism. One of the first times that I remember truly expressing myself in a leadership capacity was in high school. Inspired by the rock band U2, I founded an Amnesty International chapter—a high school chapter—whose main purpose would be to organize and run letter-writing campaigns among my fellow students to free prisoners of conscience overseas. Together, we orchestrated dances and fundraisers and a myriad of activities to help liberate people halfway around the world, people who had been imprisoned for their ideas. Even as a teenager, the wrongness of this idea—jailing people because of what they thought—burned inside of me until I had to take action.

So when I think about leadership, I remember these stories, and I think about how an evolution beyond fear-driven consciousness has been the common thread throughout my whole journey. Pegged as an old soul from a young age, I believe I volunteered to come here in order to help guide others and avoid the pitfalls of a life driven by fear rather than love.

Team Building: Embracing the Unorthodox

Every competent leader knows that she, individually, is only as good as her team is collectively. In the high seas (and even the calmest of waters), all oars must row together in harmony to move forward. So when focusing on the various components of leadership, I think my commitment to my own essential self and ongoing evolution becomes a quintessential barometer of how effectively the organization is going to function. In this way, I would say that my leadership style focuses on helping everyone get into their best alignment, even if that means leaving the company to pursue a more aligned organization or profession. It is important to me that my employees know I am here to empower them, that I am actively rooting for each one of them to align themselves with what makes them the happiest, and that I actively and compassionately give them the permission to follow through on those goals.

I believe this extends into the personal lives of my team as well as their professional lives. If things are not aligned with their truth for the rest of their lives, due to cultural conditioning and other distortional influences, the higher vibrational coordinates of my company will initiate much-needed changes to realign them to their pre-birth intentions. Part of how I show up as a leader for my team is in making sure that they know I am just as invested in their personal success as their professional success.

In college, I rowed crew. On each boat, there are eight seats, plus the coxswain. What I remember about that experience was there were times when you would realize quite suddenly that even though you may have only moved one seat forward or backward, or even laterally, for whatever reason, you would become aware of how incongruent you were for that particular spot. In other words, putting people in their respective "right places" was the penultimate job of our coach. He would play nautical musical chairs with us until everyone had found just the right seat—their own personal best fit. Similarly, I think an important component of motivating your team in the long term has to do with continuously striving to make sure everyone finds their own "right seat."

Another facet of keeping my team motivated and aligned with the company's mission, as well as their own personal missions, can be...well, a bit unconventional. Given that my job demands I work closely with the metaphysical aspects of the universe, the idea seems very normal to me, but it's not always viewed that way by others. Here is how it works:

I work in terms of light quotient. So we have all heard of an intelligence quotient; we've even heard about an emotional quotient, right? Well, light quotient is probably just the next set of advanced physics that modern science will soon discover. Most light is measured in terms of what is and is not visible by the human eye. However, there are infinitely more wavelengths to light than what we are capable of perceiving. In our purest form, we are a field of light-filled consciousness. And so part of how I strengthen our relationship as a cohesive team is that I've created a specific in-person retreat for my employees. The primary focus of this retreat is to construct an ideal environment to shift the light quotient. How can we think about this in laymen's terms? Have you ever entered a room before and felt the presence of someone, positive or negative, before you had even spoken to them? Has a particular group of people in your life ever seemed to emit an aura of heaviness or downtrodden spirit that you were able to detect without speaking? What you were experiencing, without even realizing it, was a low light quotient.

The primary function of my team retreat (and client retreats) is to help people enter an environment where they can intentionally displace density and distortion in their bioenergy field. What I find amazing about these experiences is that when my team collectively enters this metaphysical space, it is rare that we do not suddenly have access to new information and ideas about how to solve problems. It's kind of like how Einstein proposed the theory that you can't solve a problem with the same level of thinking that created it. Our modus operandi, then, is to open new vistas, drop the illusion of limitation and lack, and expand our awareness to the possibility of new solutions and innovative ideas.

Alternative Strategies to Becoming a Highly Effective Leader

Somewhat ironically, my career aspirations initially saw me trying to pursue a career in paleoanthropology—the study of human evolution. I say this is ironic because the work I do today, on the metaphysical plane, while not academically parallel, has the same clarity of purpose: I want to help our species evolve through the next evolution.

In coaching our clients, one of the most underrated and underutilized assets that I encourage other leaders to tap into is their breath. Specifically, the use of very focused, intentional breathing to move through and open blocked energy centers within the body. Often, people carry generational trauma without ever realizing it. We are shouldering the expectations, hopes, dreams, and experiences of our parents, our grandparents, and even our great-grandparents. Deliberate and daily breath work is a core tenet of my leadership self-development. Learning to use breath work to cleanse your bioenergetic field is a direct path to unearthing your authentic, essential self, a self-sovereign state in which the most empowering leadership is found.

The second strategy I employ to become a more effective leader is to cultivate the practice of speaking my own truth. This is often far easier said than done. Due to the intensity and frequency of the cultural conditioning we receive in childhood and thereafter, it is perilously easy to forget the sound of your own internal voice, and once you've lost that, there's not much hope for you to lead in any manner of authenticity. I like to say that being able to *speak* your truth follows naturally after being able to *know* your truth clearly. This, of course, implies some level of self-reflection and self-awareness. In my view, speaking your truth never has to be more complicated than saying "yes" when you want to say yes, saying "no" when you want to say no and understanding why each of those answers resonates with you and holding true to that discernment. Blindly following the lead of others is how we all end up marching off a cliff without seeing it. So speaking your truth is really about sourcing your information from the inside out.

Finally, it is my belief that a highly effective leader infuses his or her efforts with love as the driving force rather than fear. The wisdom of love was lost over time and has become an expendable commodity; it's tossed aside in favor of other, shinier objects or else deemed as metaphysical nonsense. But from a physics perspective, the vibrational frequency of operating from a center of love is the most expansive position you can hold within this universe. Because "love" as we define it is comprised of the most comprehensive set of frequencies, leveraging this natural force as a leader allows you to see so much more in terms of ideas, innovative solutions, and clear pathways to your goals. A great leader must have the ability to transcend fear-based thinking.

When we operate from a place of fear, we contract rather than expand. We try to control the process from what I would say is our least intelligent aspect: our minds. Our heart is built to be the most expansive if we work with it in that way. It's like a supercomputer capable of changing the vibrational output of our entire being. Conversely, the leader who is consistently plagued by fear and worry is only acting to create more chaos in their environment. Their sight is limited to a very narrow interpretation of a reality that is actively rearranging itself.

Final Thoughts on Leading With Love

If I could turn back the hands of time, there are a number of things that would have been useful to know as I was figuring out my own path. Though I wouldn't change a single step I took—as each step brought me to where I am today—I'd be remiss if I didn't also say that there is wisdom in experience. From that perspective, here are some final thoughts to guide you as you continue on your own experience towards luminary leadership:

You can't get this wrong. There is no failure. There is, of course, the mainstream definition of failure, wherein a collection of experiences defied your expectations: you did not "meet the goal." However, every opportunity that goes awry or does not unfold as you had imagined is only a failure when you decide it is so. A more constructive way to view these experiences is that you only have two possible outcomes: you succeed in your endeavor, or you gain experience from trying. Failure is a personal judgment that YOU decide to thrust upon your experiences. Thus, there is really no such thing as failure if you decide not to accept it that way.

A willingness to face the truth of how you feel is the most important contract you can make with yourself. It is impossible to make good decisions—decisions that are in alignment with your values and ethics as a leader—if those choices are not grounded in honesty with oneself. Most of us were taught to avoid the full truth of what we feel, leading to all sorts of misalignment and dis-ease with the reality we ended up in. You can reverse this distortion by being willing to see the truth of what your emotions have been trying to tell you all along.

Lead yourself with love. No matter what. Every day we are faced with a plethora of choices to make, choices that no one else can decide for us. From the moment you wake up in the morning, you have a choice in what you choose to think. You can choose to lead yourself with love and self-compassion, or you can allow the choice to be made for you, informed by unconscious, negative, ancestral, and cultural conditioning. The benefit of leading with love is that it can act as a fantastic foundation for all that you do. If you open your heart center and lead with love, you will very quickly discover if there are any facets of your life that are not in alignment with your true purpose. The biggest regrets we face at the end of life are the things we didn't dare to do. Follow your heart, fear less, and love more!

The Journey Never Ends

Kumar Parakala

Kumar R. Parakala is a global business leader and technology entrepreneur with over two decades of experience building high-growth businesses in global consulting firms. He currently serves as the president of GHD Digital, a business founded after the global professional services GHD acquired his award-winning company Technova. Earlier in his career, Kumar worked with KPMG, leading its global technology advisory practice and serving in executive leadership and managing partner roles.

With over five hundred board director briefings as a trusted advisor and nonexecutive director, Kumar works extensively with publicly listed boards and CEOs and served in nonexecutive director roles.

Respected among the foremost thought leaders, President Clinton invited Kumar to the Clinton Global Initiative. Ranked in the top 50 most influential technology leaders, ACS inducted him into its Hall of Fame, conferring him with the Honorary Life Membership (HLM). As an international digital business transformation and innovation expert, Forbes, Wall Street Journal, AFR, Financial Times, *ABC, CNBC, and several media outlets featured his thought leadership. When not at work, he pursues his passion as a jazz musician.*

From Small Towns to Global Markets

Life began in India in a small village of fewer than four thousand people. My parents, grandfathers, and ancestors lived in small villages for about a thousand years or more. My father became the first ever graduate in the family, which changed life's trajectory for his children and grandchildren. He was a civil engineer with a government job, so we moved around a lot, growing up in small towns.

India is a highly competitive culture of over one billion people, so it was clear to me from an early age that success was paramount. Academic failure is not an option. It was also clear that no matter how good you thought you were, you could always do better. I don't mind admitting that I struggled to find my place in the world during my early years. How do I fit in? Am I good enough? Do I have what it takes to succeed?

In the early nineties, I moved to Australia, where I lived for almost thirty years. It was there that I started a new life. From humble beginnings with only a few dollars in my pocket, I enjoyed a newfound freedom and, with a sense of adventure, looked to the future with confidence. I fell in love with Australia and its people. My friends and colleagues had strong values of humility, authenticity, and fairness. They had self-deprecating humor and a healthy disdain for authority. Mostly, I came to appreciate their fierce loyalty. As an immigrant and person of ethnic background and color, rejection was common on the grounds of "cultural fitment," even for highly qualified professionals of color. At that time, there were almost no leaders of my background in the business world to look up to or turn to for guidance, but a few mainstream leaders were remarkably supportive and became my sponsors.

I realized that I couldn't change discrimination on my own when it happens, but what I could do was change the way I thought about discrimination. At least this was within my control. I chose to view every opportunity missed and regular failures as an opportunity to learn and try again. I chose to imagine a bold life, full of possibilities and extraordinary accomplishments. I chose to focus on what was core to who I am—a deep sense of the need to care for people, build relationships, and change things for the greater good.

Labeling challenges as "growth" opportunities has become a recurring theme in my career. It's how I've navigated failures and come out intact—and even stronger—at the other end. I believe it is how I have managed to get to where I am today. I share some of these successes below, not to glorify my achievements, but to prove that it is possible to overcome perceived shortcomings. If I can become a leader, I truly believe anyone can. It's a mindset.

My first big break was as the chief information officer (CIO) for the Queensland Government—the youngest to hold the role. It resonated with my belief in public duty, and I served three government agencies as CIO. I received the Premier's Leadership Excellence Award in 2000.

This led to a fifteen-year career at KPMG. A co-founding global executive and partner of the Technology Advisory practice in 2005, we built a $2 billion consulting business of twelve thousand people worldwide. I was the one of first few Australian partners of color—probably the only one for many years—and held several global leadership roles consulting for various Fortune 500, FTSE 200, and ASX

200 companies. I can't thank some of the most amazing people I met who enabled my success enough, including the global chairman, global managing partners, CEOs, and key leaders of Australian business. While still at KPMG, I was elected National President and Chairman of the Board by twenty thousand members of the Australian Computer Society. I became a national spokesperson for the industry and advisor to federal and state ministers. My public profile led to various invitations, from Former President Bill Clinton to join the Clinton Global Initiative, Forbes Global CEO Forums, and thought leadership in print and broadcast media worldwide.

I founded my own company, Technova, in 2015. A digital advisory firm, it was awarded the ACS Digital Disruptor International Award in 2016 and was acquired by GHD the following year. I was given the rare opportunity to lead the formation of a new business unit within GHD, an amazing employee-owned global engineering and professional services firm with over ten thousand people. At GHD, I am working with some of the best people I have ever met professionally—humble, incredibly talented, high-integrity human beings making the world a better place.

Established in 2018, the GHD Digital team has grown to over six hundred people in less than four years, making it one of the fastest-growing corporate startups of its kind and a leader in the engineering and construction industry. Strongly aligned to diversity and inclusion principles, we have 50 percent women on our global leadership team and have delivered more than two thousand client engagements in FY2022. I'm proud of what we have achieved to date as a team, but there is much more to do.

Today, more than ever, we need new leaders—leaders who can think differently and keep pace with a world that is changing so fast post-COVID. Our society and organizations need leaders with the skills to help us thrive in the face of relentless change, volatility, uncertainty, and complexity.

There Are No "Born Leaders"

While on the public speaking circuit, I've had the privilege of engaging with numerous prominent leaders from all walks of life, from Barack Obama to John Howard, Angela Merkel to Shimon Peres, and Bill Gates to Deepak Chopra. Despite their obvious talents, I believe there are no "born leaders." They have worked hard for their success.

Someone much smarter than me once wrote this:

> When we are foolish, we want to conquer the world.
> When we are wise, we want to conquer ourselves.

The following seven traits have served me well over my leadership journey of the last thirty-plus years:

1. Having a Bold Vision

Developing a bold vision that inspires others, passionately advocating for it, and working with people to turn it into reality have been the centerpiece of my leadership journey. In all my roles, I could see opportunities that others could not. Some see me as a "big-picture" thinker, but it's not enough to simply see the bigger picture; it is also critical to inspire people and create a shared vision to influence senior leaders and motivate them to act.

A bold vision needs passion and a willingness to take major business and career risks that many are not brave enough to take. It takes throwing oneself into the metaphorical "deep end" in "sink or swim" situations and learning from painful failures and mistakes.

I have taken many personal and professional risks, perhaps more than most. I've deliberately stepped into unknown situations to create opportunities to improve myself as a leader. Changing jobs, launching new ventures, and accepting ambitious assignments are all examples of the risks I took to help me grow. Risk-taking created some hardships, but it also led to great successes. It was all worth it, no regrets! The challenges forced me to bring my best by experimenting, innovating, and adapting. I learned rapidly from my errors and failures. For bold leaders, "adversity is the fertilizer for growth."

2. A Compelling Higher Purpose

Early in my career, I recognized that higher purpose is not about financial gain but about shared aspirations to make a difference—a positive impact on an individual, organization, community, or society as a whole. My purpose was to create businesses that could offer fulfilling careers to thousands of people so their families could prosper and, in turn, generate tremendous community value.

Most recently, my higher purpose is to help leaders empower millions of people by understanding the impact of technology and innovation—how new ways of thinking and doing, enabled by technology, will allow them to reimagine and reinvent their organizations to create lasting community benefit. The higher purpose and values of the individual must be aligned to those of the organizations they serve to avoid a "values conflict." A higher purpose can be a great source of motivation.

3. Being Real and Vulnerable

In the early part of my career, I often felt that acknowledging vulnerabilities was seen as a sign of weakness. I learned this from leadership at the time. I once had a boss who would compare himself to either Batman or Superman depending on the day of the week.

As I progressed in my leadership journey, I learned to be more open and honest with people to create greater trust and stronger relationships. Sometimes, people may not like the candor, but in the long run, they know that I always "walk the talk." Being real and vulnerable with people means acknowledging my shortcomings and failures and, when necessary, seeking their help to improve how I lead. In the early days, as a minority leader of color, I would consciously try to fit in and say what I thought others wanted to hear to please them. I eventually realized that I had to be my authentic self to foster good emotional and mental well-being. Now I take pride in who I am and what I bring to the table, including my vulnerabilities, fears, authenticity, and empathy.

4. Loving My People

Grand visions don't materialize unless we have inspired people with something meaningful to unite behind. No leader can get things done alone. I believe leadership is all about enabling others to be successful. A large part of my role is to bring together a large number of people and motivate them to accomplish phenomenal outcomes that would be impossible for one individual alone. I see myself as an integrator, bringing together people with specialized skills, different views, and interests to create high-value outcomes.

Loving your people means recognizing their contributions and expressing your confidence and appreciation in their abilities. Encouragement and recognition are important for people to perform at their best and maximize their potential. It helps greatly when outcomes require persistence over time, hard work, and dealing with complex issues.

I'm a big believer in one-to-one engagement to encourage people and drive motivation. People are motivated by different things. The biggest myth in the world is that everybody is motivated by money. No amount of money in the world can replace the power of a personal "Thank you, I really appreciate it." There is real power in expressing gratitude; the more senior you are, the more you need to express it when contributors deserve it. The more leaders recognize their teams, the more motivated they are likely to be.

5. Challenging the Status Quo

Early in my career, a former boss told me that challenging the status quo is a career-limiting move. Fast-forward thirty years and I am glad I ignored his advice. In fact, I've built a successful career by challenging the status quo, which is a core strength for me. The more I worked with Fortune 500 executives, bureaucrats, and politicians, the more I realized that challenging the status quo respectfully and offering compelling new perspectives with persuasive explanations can be very powerful in influencing how others think. According to a recent study, only 3 percent of leaders constantly challenge the status quo. I've often promoted or provided incentives to those who challenge the status quo, and they haven't proved me wrong.

6. A Hunger for Learning and Self-Improvement

In today's world, abandoning old-school thinking and learning new skills is critical. Leaders need the knowledge and skills to stay relevant to the stakeholders they serve. It doesn't mean a leader must be an expert in everything they do, but they must have enough competency to get things done.

I often rigorously self-evaluate my thinking, skills, and competencies using daily self-awareness rituals. To learn, I rely upon a variety of sources including other leaders, books, and short courses. Engaging with my team members—especially the young generation—is my biggest source of inspiration and learning.

7. Never Giving Up: Building the Resilience Muscle

A leadership journey is full of challenges, some due to a specific path the leader has chosen, others due to the environment in which they operate. As much as possible, I don't let setbacks slow me down. I seek ways to overcome obstacles when things don't go as planned, which is often the case. These have included missed job opportunities on subjective criteria, unfair assessments, references to my ethnic and cultural background, and other issues not based on meritocracy but rather on human bias. I've prevailed in many situations against the odds over a sustained period, interpreting failure as a temporary event and, even when highly stressful, moving forward to change the outcome.

The Leadership Journey Is Never Over

People of all ages and backgrounds can be leaders. They need not be high up in an organizational structure. The behaviors, skills, and abilities needed to be an effective leader can always be learned, strengthened, and improved, providing that people have the motivation and desire to become better leaders. Managers manage the present while leaders are focused on the future. Leadership is not about how you can just deliver bottom-line results but how you can drive the long-term success of the people and organizations you lead. Leadership is not just limited to professional environments. Great leaders transcend the day-to-day duties of their role to benefit their people, organizations, industries, and communities. Leaders are not born; they are made. I invite you to imagine your leadership journey today and create a future where you are making a huge difference to your teams, organizations, communities, and nations.

Lighting the Path

Sharón Lynn Wyeth

ex mortem

Sharón Lynn Wyeth was an internationally recognized name expert. She could determine one's strengths, challenges, and the purpose of one's life by deciphering a person's name. Sharón created Neimology® Science, the study of the placement of the letters in a name, after fifteen years of research.

Sharón assisted HR business departments to narrow down interview candidates. She also assisted lawyers in how to present cases to judges and helps couples and families to communicate better. Sharón also created names for new businesses and new products and when people wished to change their name. She wrote several bestselling books and was a frequent guest on radio and television. www.knowthename.com. *In memoriam to her wonderful life and work.*

What Do All Leaders Have in Common?

There are many good leaders in the world. There are fewer great leaders in the world. Yet, it is rare to find a luminary leader. Luminary leaders are those who light the path for others to easily follow, and they do it with an unbridled enthusiasm and talent for their work. They lead by both power and influence. These are certain characteristics that all luminary leaders share:

1. Contracted with God
2. Talents, education, and hobbies in alignment with work being done

3. Professionals, work associates, and friends whose talents are in corresponding fields

Contracted with God

Every individual has unique strengths, talents, and challenges, which are specified within his/her contract with God. This includes the best usage of those gifts, which equate to a particular career field. So when leadership is contracted by God in a person's life path, they have a choice as to what kind of leader each chooses to become. Fueled by desire, good leaders can become great leaders, and great leaders can become exceptional leaders.

The blueprint for one's life is hidden within each person's name. Said another way, the light of their being is the light of their soul. This light's information and morality emanate from the core of one's soul and is what leads a person to excel in their specific area.

Leaders must possess true knowledge of the topic of which they are in charge. Leaders must be continually learning; looking beyond current circumstances, recognizing current functioning levels of the company, and simultaneously envisioning the potential. Both personal and professional/business mentors aid in this process. This is combined with a compassionate personality, which is sensitive to the fears and constraints of the people they are leading. Leaders must also have a clear moral code to keep their judgment authentic and unbiased. These qualities will ensure the leader retains respect.

Luminary leaders have the knowledge base to think positively and objectively in all situations. They are also careful to be respectful of others' dreams and business acumen. They do not deviate into pride by insisting on their own agenda. Likewise, their moral code prohibits them from misrepresenting their own expertise. Thus, ethics are high on the list of qualities held by luminary leaders.

Luminary leaders also hold the vision for the company, giving it quite a bit of energy and holding the space for others to grow. Employees must be stimulated to succeed and given the freedom to experiment. A degree of freedom allows inherent talent to be identified and developed. Education, training, appreciation, and rewards nurture employees to shine, ensuring that all participants in the venture, the business, and the luminary leader are successful!

Let's go back to the critical importance of knowledge. It took me fifteen years of research, followed by three years of testing to create Neimology® Science; the science of knowing how to interpret the placement of the letters in a name to know someone's personality traits and their life's purpose. Since I created the science, I know it better than anyone else. I have achieved a level of luminescence, a level of mastery of Neimology® Science. In addition, I continue to find new patterns that extend Neimology® Science even further. Luminary leaders love their subject so they continue to learn more about it. They also wish to share their knowledge by teaching what they know. Thus, I have written four books on the subject and have been a guest on nearly five-hundred radio/podcasts and/or television shows to share this informative system.

How many times has someone asked, "Why am I here?" What is my purpose? Neimology® Science answers this question beautifully and very succinctly, including the seven subsets that comprise one's overall purpose. There are other modalities that also answer these important questions.

Talents, Education, and Hobbies in Alignment with Work Being Done

Luminary leaders have innate talents, interests, and hobbies that meld into their chosen occupations. Some of my natural talents that facilitated the creation of Neimology® Science include the combination of spiritual, mathematical, relational, and linguistic intelligence. I was reared by a mother who taught us to be active spiritual seekers and a father who wanted our approach to life to be logical. I am a naturally gifted teacher and mathematician holding a bachelor of science degree in mathematics, along with a master's degree. As a people person, I love teaching all ages. I enjoy sharing my knowledge and seeing others learn. Public speaking, seminars, broadcasting, radio, and podcasting are all my forums.

I also studied psychology and sociology to better understand recurring patterns I found in names. It was important to know what causes humans to act as they do even as their name indicates their future actions. Studying these two fields allowed me to understand the challenges that were present in a person's name and how to overcome those challenges. It was also helpful to have forty years of working in our education system: twenty-nine as a teacher and eleven as an administrator.

After developing Neimology® Science, I started dabbling in esoteric methodologies like astrology, physiognomy, and handwriting analysis. Studying alternative ways of arriving at the same information became my hobby. Almost all other modalities require the other person to share information about themselves as the other modality may require a person's birthday information or a handwriting sample. It is also quite important not to get stuck in one perspective.

Hence, my friends continually present me with new ideas and/or ways of looking at what I've previously found. They share with me as I do with them.

Friends Whose Talents Are in Corresponding Fields

Luminary leaders have professional relationships and friendships that contribute to their core knowledge. Friends need to have a comparable/compatible education to support the leader. So my talents, education, and hobbies are naturally concurrent with my main body of knowledge. My professional relationships are mostly with spiritual teachers, including J. J. Dewey and Dr. Eugene E. Whitworth. My friends include Medical Intuitive Susan Klopfstein and Psychic Mediums Susan Rowlen and Melinda Vail. Each one contributes to my life so that I experience a full, rich professional and personal life. I am sharing their information at the end of the chapter so that you may also benefit from meeting them if you feel drawn to do so.

J. J. Dewey authored a series of books starting with *The Immortal*, in which he shares how to interpret the Bible for today's cultural settings.[12,13] J. J. Dewey has been my mentor since 1998. Dr. Eugene Whitworth is also a prolific writer, as he fills in gaps in the Bible with his

---

[12] J. J. Dewey, The Immortal: Books 1 & 2, 1st ed., vol. 1 (Boise, ID: Great AD-Ventures, 1998).

[13] JJ Dewey's work can be accessed at www.freeread.com, where his first book can be read for free.

well-researched books starting with *Nine Faces of Christ*.[14,15] Both have given numerous seminars, and I've sponsored both so that they could also share their knowledge with my friends. Dr. Eugene Whitworth was my personal mentor for seven years until his passing in 2004. Whitworth taught me how to meditate to reach a deeper space. I was quite disciplined and meditated twice a day, but each session felt like it was lasting hours instead of thirty minutes. I started with transcendental meditation, progressed to guided meditations with Jach Pursel, and eventually landed on Robert Monroe's methodologies.[16,17] This served me well enough until Dr. Whitworth shared his technique with me. This new technique made an hour of meditation feel like only five minutes had passed.

Susan Klopfstein is a spiritual therapist and medical intuitive who can remote-view, scanning her client's spiritual and physical bodies.[18] Then she can see where their disease state originated, in what lifetime, and release

---

[14] Eugene E. Whitworth, Nine Faces of Christ: Quest of the True Initiate, Revised Edition (Camarillo, CA: Devorrs Publications, 1980).

[15] Dr. Eugene Whitworth founded the Great Western University in the San Francisco Bay area in California to teach aspiring spiritual leaders as they earned their Ph.D. in ancient religions and learned how to raise one's consciousness. The college is now called the Great Western Brotherhood School of Sacred Studies.

[16] Jach Pursel channeled the spirit Lazarus. More information can be found at: www.onlinepsychicchat.org/psychic-biographies/psychic-jach-pursel/

[17] Robert Monroe, known as Bob to his friends, founded the Monroe Institute in Faber, VA. He coined the term OBE for Out-of-Body Experience and initiated the process known as hemi-sync technology, which teaches the two halves of the brain to synchronize.

[18] Susan Klopfstein's website is www.soulwealth.com.

the energy of the illness through all time continuums. Thus, the body has no need to recreate the disease again.

Susan Rowlen and Melinda Vail are mediums, yet they work quite differently.[19,20] Susan can assist individuals in conversing with a deceased loved one while Melinda is an evidentiary medium coming up with names and information that she hears from your loved ones. Both mediums are stunningly accurate, entertaining, insightful, and tremendously helpful to my clients who have experienced the loss of loved ones.

The real challenge when one has such talented friends is to maintain a high degree of morality and commitment to the truth without deviating into jealousy for others who have incredible talents and skills and may be more business savvy. When people nurture their own gifts and skills, they tend to be less jealous of others. Luminary leaders understand that all may shine and are committed to making that happen.

---

[19] Susan Rowlen's website is www.susanrowlen.com.

[20] Melinda Vail's website is www.melindavail.com.

Kaizen Leadership

Rick Yvanovich

Rick Yvanovich is a USA Today *and* Wall Street Journal *bestselling author, executive coach, serial entrepreneur, techie, Brit, baby boomer, and professional bean counter (hence FCMA, CGMA, FCPA). Rick has spent more than forty years in supermarkets, accounting profession, breweries, newsagents, defense manufacturing, IT, talent, F&B, property development and BP, living in the UK, China, Singapore, Switzerland, and Vietnam.*

Posted to BP China as Finance Manager, Rick then relocated to BP Vietnam in 1990 making him likely the longest Brit and one of the most seasoned expats in Vietnam. He served as Board Member of BritCham Vietnam, Chairman Industry Advisory Committee RMIT Vietnam, CIMA assessor, and founder/co-founder/CFO/investor/advisor of multiple start-ups (not all of which have failed!).

Rick is an active promoter of CIMA and a regular speaker on talent, accounting, ERP, technology, digital transformation, project management, doing business in Vietnam, UK-Vietnam and Vietnam inward investment. Rick's coaching journey includes CCMP (2018), Leaders Create Leaders (2020), Genos Emotional Intelligence Practitioner (2021), OKR Champion (2021), Ikigai Coach (2021), CCMC (2021), and CBC (2022).

Learning to Lead by First Following Others

Leadership was not something I was inherently born with. It was, I believe, something I've acquired along the way. When I was younger, I saw myself more as a follower than a leader. Although that's due to what my leadership reality looked like then, my reality has changed over the years. As I was growing up, the concept of leadership that I perceived society projected was perhaps not leadership. We learned (and were told to "shut up and do as you're told") to respect and obey our elders, both familial and societal. At times, this was frustrating as this silenced my solutions and ideas. As a self-identified "follower," I looked up to whoever I was being led by; in so doing, I began to see those qualities I wanted to acquire and those that I didn't. I perceived that leadership in the last century since the 1960s (I'm a baby boomer) was typically defined by whatever title you had following your name. To be recognized as a leader, you had to head up something: the head of a sports team, the head of a company, the head of an investment group, etc. That was my perception, and I just assumed that was leadership.

Become the kind of leader that people would follow voluntarily, even if you had no title or position.
—Brian Tracy

Today, I know you don't need a title to be a leader. You can be a leader without a title. I particularly like one saying related to understanding how and when you can define yourself as a leader: "What's leadership? Walk in any direction, stop, and turn around. Is there anybody following you?" I remember the saying, but I can't remember who said it, so I apologize for citing your words and not giving you credit. In one way, I feel that I did not acquire leadership characteristics until I was running my own company. Do you know the single most challenging thing about being at the top of the pyramid? There's no one higher up to defer to! The learning curve was huge and steep, with no standard operating procedures, no manual to read, and no one to take your cues from.

Luckily, the opportunity I had to run a business did not happen overnight. Instead, it afforded me many years of patiently watching, learning, and unconsciously preparing for the day when I would assume a similar caliber of responsibility as the mentors and coaches I looked up to. I will be the first to admit that when it comes to my journey and evolution as a leader, it began first and foremost with following others. Yet that style, too, has changed as I've learned and grown over the years. So often I think people mistake a particular leadership style as being something irrevocable, permanent, and unchanging—but nothing could be further from the truth. Growth is all about pursuing an infinite mindset; it's about allowing yourself to grow out of and into what best suits the challenges you're facing today. The person you are today is not the person you were in the past, and it's not the person you will be tomorrow or in the future as you continue to grow and evolve.

We cannot become what we want to be by remaining what we are.
—Max DePree

Today I employ a leadership style that blends coaching, consulting, and mentoring. I tend to default to coaching as I've found that people typically already have the answers within themselves. It's simply helping them unearth them. Yet, other times, I will approach as a consultant or a mentor, though I remain mindful of never trying to spoon-feed others. It's far better to instill in them independence and confidence in their abilities, as opposed to a dependence on mine.

Give a man a fish, and you feed him for a day.
Teach him how to fish, and you feed him for a lifetime.
—Lao Tzu

All this is to say that leadership, acquired or inherent, is something that I believe you grow into and grow with. Unfortunately, each decade seems to usher in a new cascade of leadership fads, standards, or techniques. Years ago, it was transformational leadership, then servant leadership; now it's turning into a coaching leadership or leader-as-coach style. Let's avoid getting mired in what kind of leadership "title" or style is *de rigueur*. Instead, it is a better practice to pick and choose à la carte those qualities and characteristics of the leaders around you that best embody and resonate with your personal and professional truths.

How Do We Define Leadership Values?

In order to stand out, we have to know what we stand for.
—Simon Sinek

Many values define us, and since each of us is unique, we also have unique values. There will be similar values within groups of like-minded people, and disparate, unrelated groups of people, less so. We know this. But what about when it comes to leadership? Are there some values that a leader absolutely *must* have? That's a difficult question. I believe that an individual *does* need to have values. Furthermore, that leader needs a set of values that align not only with their own beliefs but with their organization and the culture they are building.

At TRG International, we have six core values, and they are also in alignment with my values. Originally, we had adopted only four: passion, integrity, collaboration, and kaizen (a Japanese term designating the process of seeking continuous improvement). However, some years ago, we reflected on the changes within our company and added two more to our list: innovation and coaching culture. So let's take a closer look at each one.

Passion

Passion is one key to success. Passion for excellence: we aspire for excellence in all we do. Passion for learning: knowledge does not stand still, nor does our knowledge. We are curious, and we seek to constantly learn and understand more. We remain relevant. Our passion for achieving our goals and moving the ball forward allows us to take each day in stride.

You have to be burning with an idea, or a problem,
or a wrong that you want to right.
If you're not passionate enough from the start,
you'll never stick it out.
—Steve Jobs

Integrity

We are direct, honest, and transparent and aim always to do the right things. We say what we do, and we do what we say. Your actions must reflect the integrity of your words and vice versa. If those people who depend on you can no longer trust your words, it would be catastrophic to your continued success. As Alan Simpson once said, "If you have integrity, nothing else matters. If you do not have integrity, nothing else matters."

It is true that integrity alone won't make you a leader,
but without integrity, you will never be one.
—Zig Ziglar

Innovation

We never stop coming up with new and better ways to do things. It's as simple as that. Time does not stand still, and neither can you! As the world is ever-changing, and the systems driving our technology become increasingly advanced, as learning becomes more available and robust, there is only one option to ensure survival: adapt.

The definition of insanity is doing the same thing over and over
again, but expecting different results.
—Albert Einstein

Collaboration

People are essential to what we do, and we foster a collaborative and friendly environment where everyone is a valued partner in our success. Doors remain open to solicit and share ideas, propose initiatives, make mistakes, and suggest improvements. You never know from where the next great idea might spring, so be open-minded, which means both being open to different perspectives from others and being prepared to change your perspective.

Don't tell people how to do things, tell them what to do and let them surprise you with their results.
—Lt. Gen. George S. Patton Jr.

Coaching Culture

Coaching culture was one of our more recently adopted values. As my leadership style changed, I fully understood the value of unleashing each person's potential and ensuring their success through coaching. You can surround yourself with the greatest, most skilled set of employees you can find, but that's not enough. If you're coaching them, pouring into them and helping them achieve all they can, and making each one of them successful, you are unleashing potential.

Kaizen

Continuous improvement. Nothing is perfect; thus, we embrace and are committed to never-ending, lifelong improvement of ourselves and all we do. Daily small-scale improvements over a long time significantly impact the individual, the team, and the organization. Therefore, every day we work on ourselves. We do not aim to do the best we can; instead, we aim to do the best that can be done and seek to make it even better!

If you're not getting better, you're getting worse.
—Joe Paterno

Coaching: a Leader's Greatest Asset

Sir John Whitmore said, "Coaching is unlocking a person's potential to maximize their performance. It is helping them to learn rather than teaching them." This definition ties in with our kaizen founding principle. Anyone who assumes the mantle of leadership must be able to nurture their people to help them grow. As Lao Tzu said, "Give a man a fish, and you feed him for a day. Teach him how to fish, and you feed him for a lifetime." In this regard, I believe that there is no skill or asset more critical in a leader's arsenal than their ability to coach others.

Coaching is broad, not static, but fluid, embracing a growing set of different skills. However, to be an effective coach and to employ coaching as an additional facet of your leadership style, there are specific foundational skillsets needed:

- **Rapport**. The invisible emotional connection, the spark, the chemistry between people.
- **Empathy**. The ability to understand the thoughts, feelings, or emotions of someone else. To understand their situation, perceptions, and feelings from their point of view and to be able to communicate that understanding back to the other person. The ability to put yourself into their shoes.
- **Awareness**. The ability to recognize your perspective not just based on your experience but also on how others see you. It's about understanding your needs and desires, habits, and everything that makes you, YOU.
- **Self-Awareness**. Having a clear perception of your personality, including your strengths,

weaknesses, thoughts, beliefs, motivation, and emotions. Understanding yourself allows you to understand other people, how they perceive you, your attitude, and your responses to them in the moment.

- **Presence**. The ICF[21] calls it "coaching presence," and it's "the ability to be fully conscious and create a spontaneous relationship with the client, employing a style that is open, flexible, and confident."
- **Trust**. When you trust someone, it means that you think they are reliable, you have confidence in them, and you feel safe with them physically and emotionally. People can be open and vulnerable when they feel their psychological safety is not in question. This level of trust is a critical factor in enabling change. In addition, when you trust another person, the levels of oxytocin, the bonding hormone, increase. Brené Brown[22] created a great trust acronym called BRAVING, which I love and am introducing wherever I can:
    - **B**oundaries – You clearly define what's okay and what's not okay.

---

[21] "Educational Program: Coaching with Presence: Five Keys for Presence-Based Coaching," Coaching with Presence:
Five Keys for Presence-Based Coaching (ICF San Diego Charter Chapter), accessed August 26, 2022, https://icf- sandiego.org/event-3705894.

[22] Ava Whitney-Coulter, "Brené Brown on What It Really Means to Trust," Mindful (Mindful Communication & Such, PBC, February 9, 2021), https://www.mindful.org/brene-brown-on-what-it-really-means-to-trust/#:~:text=To%20talk%20about%20trust%2C%20Brown,t%20trust%20others%2C%20or%20ourselves.

- **R**eliability –You always do what you say you'll do.
- **A**ccountability –You own your mistakes, apologize, and fix them if possible.
- **V**ault –You don't share information or experiences that are not yours to share.
- **I**ntegrity –You choose courage over comfort. You choose what is right over what is fun, fast, or easy. And you choose to practice your values rather than simply professing them.
- **N**on-Judgment –You can ask for help without being hard on yourself, and you're not hard on others who need help.
- **G**enerosity – You extend the most generous interpretation possible to the intentions, words, and actions of others.
- **Congruence**. Having a consistent state of behavior. You do what you say, think and feel. It sounds like integrity, doesn't it?
- **Neutrality**. The ability to not make unsolicited judgments in a situation. It creates a safe place to express whatever comes up without fear of backlash or criticism. Again, it's about seeing yourself as an external observer of the situation.

PART FOUR:

FORWARD

Lessons in how we build a better future

My Leadership Journey: Lessons Learned

by Prasad S. Kodukula

Dr. Prasad S. Kodukula, PMP, PgMP, DASM, DASSM, is a PMI Fellow, thought leader, coach, inventor, and entrepreneur with more than thirty years of professional experience. He is co-founder and CEO of two companies: Kodukula & Associates, Inc., a project management coaching and consulting company; and NeoChloris, Inc., a clean energy company. He has lectured on project management, leadership, and innovation in nearly fifty countries. His experience includes every one of the eleven S&P industrial sectors and forty Fortune 100 companies (e.g., Abbott, BP, Chrysler, Dow, IBM, JPMorgan Chase, Kraft, Motorola, Stryker, United Technologies). He also teaches project management at the University of Chicago.

Prasad was recognized three times by the Project Management Institute as "Best of the Best in Project Management" with a 2020 PMI Fellow Award, 2016 Eric Jenett Project Management Excellence Award, and 2010 PMI Distinguished Contribution Award. He received prestigious awards from the USEPA and the states of Kansas and Illinois for outstanding achievements in education, training, and technology innovation. Prasad is a co-author or contributing author of ten books and more than forty articles and holds four patents.

Leadership is a journey—not an easy one, for sure. For many of us, it feels like a trek up Everest. It's treacherous and scary, yet thrilling and rewarding. At every step you take and every turn you make, there is the potential to learn something new, exciting, and rewarding. I'm grateful for the many lessons I've learned—the dos and don'ts—on my leadership journey. They helped me become a better human being as well as a leader and teacher in my professional career.

My first job after graduate school was with a startup. It's where I had my first taste of entrepreneurship and decided that I'd become an entrepreneur one day. After a couple of short corporate stints, I co-founded and became the CEO of three companies over the last twenty-five years. In one of my early companies, we patented and developed proprietary technologies in greenhouse gas mitigation, decarbonization, and biofuels. We were way ahead of the curve in climate change and sustainability. We forged a similar story in technology. We developed an "intelligent" system for monitoring water treatment plants applying AI/ML (Artificial Intelligence/Machine Learning), pattern recognition, IoT (Internet of Things), and cloud (the latter terms did not even exist then). We were recognized as the most innovative environmental technology company in the state of Illinois.

Over these entrepreneurial years, I learned a lot about business, innovation, and leadership. At the same time, I became increasingly curious about leadership as a subject of study. So I read books, listened to recordings of pundits, and attended seminars by experts. Slowly, I started to teach the subject and became a "pracdemic," a practicing academic.

Living the Dream

I was born in India and spent the first two decades of my life there. We were five siblings living in a one-room apartment with our parents. The apartment had no indoor plumbing, no running water, and no air conditioning. Finding it difficult to make ends meet, my parents sent me away to my grandmother's place where I attended high school and college.

My father was a highly principled, blue-collar worker always supporting and fighting for the little guy. My mother stayed home taking care of the children. My parents have been my role models and leadership coaches all of my life. They taught me the importance of human values in life. They epitomized authenticity, and that's probably the most important leadership lesson I learned from them. My grandmother taught me the importance of education and how it can pave the path to prosperity and uplift us from our modest lives. (No wonder I ended up with one PhD, two MAs, two bachelor's degrees, and many prestigious certifications!) The foundational values I learned from my parents and grandmother served me remarkably well for the rest of my life.

In my college years, I dreamed of coming to the United States, the land of opportunities, for advanced education and to travel the world. In my early twenties, against all odds, I was admitted to Cornell University to pursue a master's degree in Environmental Engineering. This is where I met Carl Sagan, a world-renowned astrophysicist. I was inspired by his vision. He engaged me to say a few words in my native tongue (Telugu) that were recorded on a disc placed on board Voyager spacecraft, which has traveled beyond our solar system exploring extraterrestrial intelligence in the cosmos.

Fast-forward to today. I've lived in the United States for forty-plus years, and traveled to more than fifty countries, primarily to teach project management and leadership to working professionals in global corporations. Living the dream!

My Early Leadership Lessons

As I embarked on my first leadership role, I thought my superior technical skills would make me an effective leader. But I was in for a surprise! I stumbled. I made many mistakes. I quickly learned a few important leadership "don'ts."

Don't Do It Yourself, Harness the Power of Your Team

A mistake I made in my early leadership years was doing a lot of the "work" myself. Most novice leaders—especially coming from a technical background like me, and even some experienced ones—are guilty of this mistake. As a leader, your job is to get it done through your team. Delegate the work. Share your vision. Inspire them. Ask for their input. Provide them with the resources and tools they need. Be a coach, guide, and a mentor. If you think you work better, cheaper, and faster (and if that's true), you can multiply yourself through effective delegation and leadership.

Don't Just Manage, but Lead

One of my early mentors taught me that leadership and management are different. The former involves formulating a long-term vision, developing strategy, setting direction, building relationships, inspiring and influencing the team, coaching, mentoring, nurturing new leaders, and making a positive impact. Management, on the other hand, is about producing short-term results; developing and implementing plans; organizing and executing tactical activities; and making products, processes, and operations more efficient. Not every great manager can become a great leader. While there's some overlap between the two, leadership warrants a different skill set. As Peter Drucker famously said, "Leadership is about effectiveness (doing the right things) and management is about efficiency (doing things right)." I'm amazed that even many experienced business executives spend most of their time managing rather than leading.

Don't Have a Fixed Mindset, Be an Adaptive Leader

There are leadership styles galore: authentic, laissez-faire, servant, situational, transformational, etc. Countless textbooks have been written on each one of them. All these styles are valuable. But remember, no one style fits all. This is especially true as you move up in the organizational hierarchy and are faced with increasingly diverse stakeholders. Plus, as the business environment is changing from simple and complicated to complex and chaotic, you need to adjust your leadership style. True, we all have our dominant style that we feel comfortable with, but it may not be effective with everybody and in every business context. We need to adapt. The right style for the right person and the right context!

Don't Ignore People, Make Them First and Foremost

The biggest challenge in my earlier leadership days was working with people and understanding how to balance relationships versus results. My focus used to be on being organized, improving processes, meeting milestones, completing projects on budget, enhancing the company's bottom line, etc. People were not exactly part of my leadership equation. At my first performance appraisal, my boss said, "The customers love what you're delivering for them, but your team members hate you." It was one of those "Aha!" moments for me. He said my job was to lead people—not just manage "things." Leadership is about putting people first, empowering them to achieve great results, listening to them, probing for better understanding, showing empathy and compassion, asking for input, involving them in problem solving, building positive relationships, and so on. It's all about leading with humanity, something I learned from my parents.

Don't Assume People Are Motivated by the Same Things

A common myth is that money alone motivates people. Many studies have shown that it's not true. Don't get me wrong—who doesn't like a fat paycheck? But I've found that people are willing to compromise for other things: flexible hours, health care benefits, challenging work, opportunities for learning and growth, better working conditions, a boss who treats them with respect, a purpose behind their work, and so on. Although these were motivating factors for many even before the pandemic, they have become much more important since. Many people are quitting their jobs in a phenomenon dubbed the "great resignation" because they cannot find what's important for them at work. As leaders, how do we know what motivates our team members? For starters, why not ask them? More importantly, listen. You'll need to use multiple motivational strategies. Apply the right strategy for the right person for the right occasion.

New Lessons for the Post-Covid Era

More leadership lessons have emerged for me in recent years, especially during the pandemic. New business and technology trends that started even before the pandemic have become starker, warranting more tools in our leadership tool kit. If we consider luminary leadership for the post-Covid era as a stool with three legs, those legs will represent three key domains—namely, people, business, and technology. I've already discussed the people domain in an earlier section. Post-Covid, "putting people first" has become more important than ever. Below I'll share a few leadership "dos" related to business and technology.

Become Digitally Savvy

Business is digital. Digital is business. They're inextricably linked. If you think you need an MBA to run a business, what degree should you have to understand the digital landscape? Many leaders think they know Digital 101 and that's good enough. But as you move up on the corporate ladder, you need to consider Digital 501. If you believe digital is a cost function, and you can just delegate it to your IT department or CIO, you're likely to be in for a big surprise in the post-Covid era. Digital-savvy leaders don't do digital transformation just because everybody else is doing it. Instead, they see it as a competitive advantage and utilize it as a strategic differentiator. Mark Andreessen, a Silicon Valley visionary and a high-profile venture capitalist, recently commented in a McKinsey & Co. interview, "Find the smartest technologist in the company and make them the CEO."

Build an Agile Organization

The pace of change around us is increasing at dizzying speed. Organizations have no choice but to transform. In the old days, a senior leader might successfully complete a transformation, earn laurels, write a book, and coast along. But today you must deal with one transformation after another. The speed of change is driving organizations into a state of perpetual transformation. To thrive in this state, you must build an agile organization. So what goes on your to-do list? Forge shared purpose. Break down organizational silos. Empower your teams. Improve communication. Pivot swiftly, when needed. Speedup decision making. Fail fast and learn fast. Build resilience. Be flexible. Adapt and evolve.

You don't need to look for lessons from twenty-first century tech pioneers. Corning—a Fortune 500 company founded in 1871 and located in its namesake remote town in upstate New York—shifted its focus in a series of transformations driven by innovations from encasements for Thomas Edison's incandescent lamps to PYREX® cookware, silicones, cathode ray tubes, TV picture tubes, optical fibers, LCDs, and smartphone glass covers through a series of transformations, thanks to the luminary leadership at the helm.

Plow Into the Stakeholder Iceberg

The "shareholder capitalism" school of thought thrived for many decades but came under attack, especially in the aftermath of the 2008/09 Great Recession. The new model is stakeholder capitalism. It may be controversial but is gaining momentum. According to this model, shareholders are at the tip of the stakeholder iceberg. Digging deeper, you'll find other stakeholders whom leaders cannot afford to ignore. In 2019, 181 CEOs of major corporations, as part of the Business Roundtable, redefined the purpose of a corporation to serve not only the shareholders but also other stakeholders including customers, employees, suppliers, and communities. Howard Schultz—who built Starbucks as a global brand and led the company twice as CEO and came back after retirement for his third stint in early summer of 2022—proclaimed that shareholder value is no longer the rule. He promised to focus on employees, cafes, and customers, not shareholders.

Senior leaders were able to get away with keeping mum on hot-button issues. Not so today, primarily because of the "Me Too" and George Floyd movements. There's a heightened pressure on leaders to address racial, social, and cultural issues head on. ESG (Environmental, Social, Governance), DEIA (Diversity, Equity, Inclusion, Accessibility), and LGBTQ+ are not just buzzwords; they're bold movements sweeping across the country and showing up at the corporate doorstep. Early in 2022, Walt Disney's CEO Bob Chapek had no choice but to publicly oppose Florida's controversial "Don't Say Gay" bill and face political backlash. You need to be super savvy to address a sensitive political issue without sounding like an activist on either side of the political spectrum.

Embrace VUCA

We are living in a VUCA (Volatile, Uncertain, Complex, Ambiguous) world, primarily driven by globalization and technology and recently shaken up by the pandemic. For a mediocre leader, it's a world full of risks. But for a luminary leader, it's a world of opportunities. To navigate through the VUCA world, you must proactively prepare by creating organizational readiness, forging agility, molding a robust culture, and building a resilient organization. You need to channel your resources to focus on the critical few initiatives rather than the trivial many. Make fast decisions to pivot to new strategies. Terminate projects that no longer align with those strategies and move the resources to those that do.

That's exactly what Airbnb's CEO Brian Chesky did when his company was on the brink of collapse towards the end of spring 2020 due to the pandemic. In the following months, he led the company towards a blockbuster IPO. Recounting his journey through the pandemic, Chesky commented in a *Wall Street Journal* interview, "I didn't know I'd make ten years' worth of decisions in ten weeks."[23]

Promote New Ways of Working

Covid made the relationship between business and technology stronger than ever. The nature of work and where and how people want to work is dramatically different today. Increasingly, workers want to be untethered

---

[23] Christie Hemm Klok, "How Airbnb Pulled Back from the Brink," The Wall Street Journal (Dow Jones & Company, October 12, 2020), https://www.wsj.com/articles/how-airbnb-pulled-back-from-the-brink-11602520846.

from an office. Work from home (WFH) is old news. How about work from anywhere (WFA)? Remote work policies are front and center in American corporations.

Leaders need to promote effective ways of working to navigate this new remote work world. "Putting people first and foremost" is even more important to lead and manage what Rajesh Gopinathan, CEO of Tata Consulting Services, a global IT consulting company, calls "talent on the cloud." Apple had egg on its face when it had to reverse its return-to-work and remote work policies—more than once—as many workers, including high-profile senior managers, were quitting.

Keep It Simple and Make It Easy

This has been my mantra for a long time. Today's evolving technologies such as AI/ML, blockchain, cloud, IoT, mobile, quantum computing, robotics, and Web 3.0 are complex. Recent surveys have consistently shown that most digital transformation projects are failing—even in digitally savvy industries such as high tech, media, and telecom. One of the keys to increase the success rate is effective communication by leadership.

As complexity increases, leaders need to double down on making things simpler to understand and easier to work with. Start with a clear definition of the purpose of the transformation—WHY are we doing it? Provide clarity of goals and benefits. Share simplified rollout plans. Enhance employee engagement. Ensure organization-wide involvement. Empower teams. Use multi-channels for communications. Avoid management speak. Be authentic, and speak from your heart. Microsoft's CEO Satya Nadella is one of the greatest communicators in business today.

He epitomizes the people-first principle. His luminary leadership transformed Microsoft from becoming irrelevant to a force to be reckoned with.

I hope that you're building your leadership mindset, skillset, and toolset to make the journey up Everest. Yes, it'll be long and arduous. But I guarantee you'll have a lot of fun!

The Human Side of Leadership

Alina Okun

Alina Okun is a former corporate executive turned entrepreneur, angel investor, and advisor. She works on projects at the intersection of Web 3.0 and the future of work, exploring new business models of organizational design, innovative ways of leading teams, and meaningful career paths where work and life align.

Alina has a Doctorate in Strategy and Innovation, an MBA in Entrepreneurial Studies, and a BBA in Public Accounting. She is a Certified Public Accountant and Chartered Global Management Accountant. To learn more about Alina and many of her projects, connect with her at https://www.linkedin.com/in/alinaokun.

"Just an analyst"is how a senior leader referred to another employee early in her career. It was as if he considered the person a peasant while he was royalty. At that moment, she decided to never treat another employee as less than human, especially because of their title.

"Human" Leadership

Even though I held leadership positions starting in elementary school, I never thought much about wanting to be a leader or leading teams. Instead, I was always curious about organizational environments that produced remarkable results. What made them different from other places?

I majored in accounting because I wanted to understand how business works, and accounting is the language of business. My goal was to lay a solid foundation on which I could build my career. In my first ten years out of college, I explored different companies and job opportunities, discovering different corporate cultures along the way.

During that time, I realized the leader of my team was far more important to my happiness at work than my day-to-day responsibilities. Regardless of company policies and procedures, the departmental leader had the power to change those rules for the benefit or detriment of their team.

As I moved into leadership roles and started to build my own teams, I drew on the leadership styles of the dozen leaders I had observed throughout my career. Those experiences helped me develop my own leadership style, which I call *Human Leadership*. Human leaders exhibit values not often seen in a traditional corporate environment:

- Shared Purpose: An alignment of leaders' and employees' values
- Social Support: A safe place for employees to propose novel ideas
- Inclusiveness: An environment where everyone's voice is heard
- Recognition: A system that makes employees feel valued

Leadership is work. It is thinking through, defining, and establishing the organization's mission and then communicating it clearly to everyone else. Leadership is about setting goals and priorities, maintaining standards, and making compromises. Leadership is a responsibility, not a rank or privilege. Leadership requires trust and people's belief that a leader means what he or she says. Without it, no one will follow, and by definition, a leader is someone who has followers.

Human leadership goes much further than that. Human leaders understand that employees are seeking a workplace that values them for who they are, allows them to bring their true selves to work, and rewards authenticity. People are looking for leaders who prioritize the humanity of leadership, demonstrate hard and soft power, and cultivate open, transparent, and inclusive work environments. This type of human leadership helps employees reach their full potential, which, in turn, contributes to the overall growth of an organization.

Meaningful Work

Human leadership is only one part of the equation. As I kept observing work environments that produced remarkable results, I noticed employees at those companies were engaged in meaningful work.

Workhuman® Analytics & Research Institute published a study revealing that employees across all age groups consider meaningful work the most important aspect of their job. Meaningful work is more important than positive company culture, a supportive manager, and even compensation. The survey found that employees were four times more likely to report loving their job when they had a sense of meaning and purpose at work.

Meaningful work connects the day-to-day responsibilities with a greater company mission that is aligned with the individual's personal values, creating a shared purpose between an employer and employees. Meaningful work formed on trust, respect, recognition, gratitude, autonomy, and equity creates a human-focused environment that improves engagement, retention, recruitment, and performance. When I dug deep into research, I discovered six principles that lead to more meaningful work:

- Managers regularly engage with direct reports and have a good sense of what is important to them.
- Employees' opinions on important issues are sought and valued.
- Organizations have a culture in which people collaborate rather than compete with one another.
- Everyone in the organization is treated with respect and dignity.
- Organizations have an environment of community and friendship.
- Rewarding and recognizing employees' hard work are important parts of the culture.

Motivation

When I started to build my first team, I was interested in understanding what motivates people. Realizing that every person has a unique personality and a distinct set of personal circumstances, I wanted to know how to motivate each team member fairly and consistently while respecting their individuality. I could not think of a better person to learn from than Daniel Pink, and I quickly purchased his book *Drive: The Surprising Truth About What Motivates Us.*[24] The findings in the book were remarkable.

---

[24] Daniel H. Pink, Drive: The Surprising Truth About What Motivates Us (New York City, NY: Riverhead Books, 2011).

Most organizations still do not understand what motivates people. Many leaders have outdated views rooted in management philosophy that originated over a hundred years ago. I will never forget when an HR professional told me that the goal of each organization is to get as much from each employee as possible while paying them as little as possible. He cited Henry Ford as the source of his insight. While what this individual said was not technically wrong, that was not the statement of a leader.

I wanted to look past the external motivation approach of the Industrial Revolution and the "carrots and sticks" or "rewards and punishment" management practices. I became a firm believer that intrinsic motivation leads to higher performance, and my goal was to create conditions for my team to do their best work. I made it a priority to get to know each person and understand what was important to them so I could motivate them in a way that was right for them.

Controllers vs. Learners

I enjoyed learning about motivation, but I also wanted to take my leadership skills to the next level. I believe reading books is one of the best strategies for becoming a more effective leader.

In his book *Conscious Business: How to Build Value through Values*, Fred Kofman identified two types of people in business: controllers and learners.[25] The leadership styles of each are dramatically different. One type will sound familiar, as it will be the kind of person we are accustomed

[25] Fred Kofman, Conscious Business: How to Build Value Through Values, Annotated Edition (Boulder, CO: Sounds True, 2006).

to seeing in the business world. The other will seem uncommon, and that was the type of leader I wanted to be.

Controllers think they know everything: how things are, how they should be, and what everyone should be doing. They stake their self-worth and self-esteem on being right. They claim that their opinions are "the truth" and impose their views on others. If someone poses a different opinion, controllers immediately argue that whoever disagrees with them is wrong. Controllers rarely listen to others.

Controllers employ a command-and-control management style, asking few questions and giving many orders. They always want to prove that their perspective is correct because it is a matter of worth to them. Their ontological arrogance blinds them from seeing other people's perspectives out of fear that they will be disproved, destroying their self-confidence in the process. They do not separate their identity from their opinions. If someone disagrees with their opinion, they see it as a threat to their image and self-esteem.

The other type of leader is a learner. An American philosopher Eric Hoffer once said: "In times of change, the learners will inherit the Earth while those attached to their old certainties will find themselves beautifully equipped to deal with a world that no longer exists." Learners are curious, open, and inquisitive. They invite others to share their opinions so everyone can learn from each other.

The opposite of ontological arrogance is ontological humility. Ontological humility is a belief that your view may not be the objective truth, and the perspectives of others may be equally valid. People with ontological humility recognize that we can look at the world in many different ways, and each approach has its blind spots.

I am a lifelong learner. When I started to work on my doctoral dissertation, we were instructed to take an unbiased approach to the subject of our research and ensure we had a 360-degree view of the topic. That meant considering different perspectives. The same applies when leading a team. Although we all live in one objective world, the way we see it is colored by our own experiential realities. Our perceptions are conditioned by our experiences. Our diverse backgrounds make our experiential realities dramatically different from others.

Inspiration

The best compliment I ever received was when someone said to me, "This is so inspiring," after I shared how I think about work. It is not just about me. Leaders who can inspire their employees give them a sense of purpose and meaning that goes far beyond external incentives. Inspired employees are more productive, more innovative, and more creative. They help to make stronger companies and stronger economies.

We are drawn to leaders and companies that excel at expressing their beliefs. Individuals who share those beliefs feel a sense of belonging and organizational loyalty. That sense of belonging makes them feel safe, special, and not alone. My favorite part of leadership is having a vision of the world that does not yet exist and communicating that vision to inspire others to follow.

Wrap-Up

If I had one departing message to someone who's about to or just recently started their leadership journey, I would tell them to view employees as human beings rather than human resources, a term that utterly lacks humanity at its core. Immanuel Kant, a nineteenth-century German philosopher, said we should never treat human beings as tools. These humanistic principles are critically important today.

The shift from the Second and Third Industrial Revolutions—which focused on productivity, efficiency, and value extraction—to the Fourth Industrial Revolution requires a new leadership approach. In a bureaucracy, employees are merely instruments or resources employed to develop products and services. Bureaucracies were designed to be dehumanizing, eliminating any personal, emotional, or irrational aspects. In such an environment, employers are constantly seeking ways to get more and more out of employees to serve their organization better.

The Fourth Industrial Revolution embraces innovation, creativity, and value creation from learning and adapting faster than the competition. This kind of environment demands a leadership style that inspires human potential.

If you want to learn how to be an effective leader, study people like Satya Nadella, CEO of Microsoft. Nadella and, because of him, Microsoft are driven by a sense of empathy and a mission to empower others. Empathy is intrinsic to connecting and empowering humans, and as technology disrupts an ever-increasing amount of our daily lives, empathy will become even more valuable. Nadella believes that we develop empathy through our own life's ups and downs. His goal is to place empathy at the center of everything he does. One of his core beliefs is that leadership is about bringing out the best in every person.

Ultimately, leaders should inspire, drive change and personal growth, and challenge conventional thinking. A company grows if employees grow individually in their roles and their lives. What I am proud of the most as a leader is developing employees and seeing them excel in their future roles, whether they stay at the same company or move on to another organization.

Leadership Is Only Half the Equation

Eric McDermott

Eric's unique brand of visual storytelling has quickly catapulted him to social media influencer, amassing more than 250,000 social media followers in a little over a year. His content helps folks reach for what's next in their careers, teams, and finances. A bestselling author, Eric ignites audiences internationally. He delivers keynotes and workshops, in-person and through his visually engaging vNote® virtual presentations, ideal for remote and hybrid teams.

Eric currently leads teams across three enterprises and draws upon twenty-five years of team leadership in an array of settings, including:

- *Start-ups and established businesses*
- *Small businesses and large organizations*
- *Nonprofits and for-profits*
- *Public and private*
- *In-person, remote, and hybrid*
- *Domestic and international*

To access Eric's content, online courses, workshop topics, books, Forbes® *articles and more, visit* https://nextpectations.com/vip.

Half the Equation, but All the Accolades?

Leadership gets so many of the societal accolades, but by itself, leadership is like one hand clapping. What if the skill a leader needs to become extraordinary isn't leadership? I have found there is another equally valuable skill.

If I ask you to imagine some of the great leaders of the past few hundred years, many of us will think of the notable social and political leaders of their time, or perhaps the iconoclastic, multinational billionaire CEOs. This has caused our study of leadership to be overwhelmingly focused on "what makes a leader a leader." Certainly, there is some merit to this approach, but something is missing when we focus only on leaders and then declare to have defined leadership. In fact, even the word *leader* may be misleading. A leader refers to an individual, yet the act of leadership itself is exceedingly social. How could we ever completely define a social act by the actions of an individual alone? We can't. In fact, it may even be harmful to truly successful acts of leadership, as it may cause people to think there is such a thing as a leader, like an immutable capability or quality. This can quickly cause people to think leadership is the only virtuous role that matters, and then in creep ego, conflict, and challenges between people to "be the leader."

The one thing ***every*** leader needs to be successful is followers. And while it garners comparatively little attention, it turns out the skill of ***followership*** may be every bit as important in creating, shaping, and amplifying great leaders as leadership.

What Physics Can Teach Us about Leadership

In physics, Einstein proved more than a century ago that time and space are connected. For example, the faster one moves through space, the slower they experience time. No longer—at least in physics—did it make sense to express space or time as distinct, and thus a new term was born: space-time. Space-time was a word that expressed that space and time were inextricably woven together, and that mentioning one without the other was an incomplete representation of what was really happening.

I propose the same is true between leadership and followership. As sure as there is one, there must be the other. All the accolades heralded upon leaders and the skill or attributes of leadership are incomplete without also recognizing, admiring, and mastering the skill of great followers and followership.

Enter Leadership-Followership. Far less catchy a phrase than space-time, but befitting nonetheless. Until we link these together in our thinking, any expression of leadership will be incomplete. Yet it's not about the leader, and it's not about the follower. Leadership is part of a social necessity, not some magical individual endowment. Every person needs help to turn out a decent life. The truth is, none of us can survive without help. And most of us spend our time working with others in family, career, and friendship to produce a better future together than we could apart.

Leadership and followership are the two most fundamental roles any of us can hold in working together to produce a better future situation than the current one we are in. But make no mistake about it: it's about the better future we can produce together, not about the role we hold in its production. If we strip away the ego, does it really matter if we lead or follow? Our cultural fascination with the role of leadership may in fact blind us to the more meaningful future outcomes we can produce together, regardless of which role we hold.

Anyone Can Lead, and Even Leaders Must Follow

With this perspective, it becomes less a concern of whether you are the leader or follower. Instead, we can see more clearly that it's about the future outcome we want to produce together. This allows us to begin to figure out what really matters in a given situation, which I have found can be addressed by beginning with two simple questions:

1. "Who among us has the better interpretation about of to produce the desired future outcome?" Enter the leader.
2. "Are the others of us willing to contribute our help to work with them to produce it together?" Enter the followers.

This allows us the ability to see leadership-followership as dynamic, not static. Picture a tall skyscraper in Manhattan, the home office of a multinational company we might read about in the news. The window washer bursts into the office of the CEO and starts telling her how to do her job. Would the CEO listen? Most likely not. However, let's change the context.

Imagine there is a fire in the building, and alarms are blaring. The window washer bursts into the CEO's office and says, "Ma'am, there is a fire, and three of the four emergency exits are engulfed in flames. I know the way to the only exit that is still clear, but we need to leave now. Follow me!" Would she listen? You bet. No one would care about their title or specific role. In that moment, the window washer has the better thinking on how to produce the desired future outcome, and even the multinational CEO will follow. And if she's a skilled leader, she will probably know how to follow very well—listening, taking direction, and supporting the window washer to clear the path as he leads.

The inverse is true as well. No matter how charismatic or convincing, would a normal person ever follow that CEO if she proposed we test the company's new, lightweight car design by running over our own feet to see if it was really lightweight enough? Probably not. Thus she would never actually become the leader because no one would willingly follow her into an outcome that was so undesirable. Whoever knows the trajectory towards a better future should drive who leads, no matter the title or specific role in an organization, which means we can all potentially lead, and as leaders, we must also learn how to yield and follow as a skill to help produce the better future together.

Steps to a Better Future Together

Leadership is social, not solo. Being a leader is not self-selection; others choose who they are willing to follow. At work, one may be the boss, but it doesn't mean they are the leader. We have all heard an expression akin to, "I have a terrible boss." Employment may come with roles where people need to do what someone tells them, but that merely requires that they comply. It does not mean they are following in a commitment to produce a better future together with that person. I suspect one of the major reasons so many employees feel disengaged in the workplace is because they feel they are working for a boss, not a leader.

Leaders need to be clear about the desired future—not just the one they want for themselves and not just the ones others want. Of course, one should gain clarity on the future intentions of anyone you intend to work closely with or hope to have follow you. However, the thing to emphasize is the future that can be built together, and that others can see their future being a part of.

Here is one simple question I ask to figure out both my idea of a desirable future, as well as others: "What has to happen for you to call *it* a success?" Swap out "it" for whatever you want to focus on:

- This meeting
- Today, this week, this year…
- This role/position

The possibilities are endless. Then consider the different stakeholders whom you'd like to build a future with, at work or in life:

- Ask this question of yourself to define your "why."
- Ask this question of others to gain clarity on what matters to them.
- Ask this question in a group setting. Give others a chance to go around and declare what they'd call "success." Use the responses to build a meaningful agenda or action plan together.

- Declare what will make a gathering a success from your point of view to galvanize help and keep folks focused. However, watch closely. If no one is following, you may need to go back to asking, not declaring.

What do you do with all this awareness of the better future you and others are after? I have found it helpful to begin looking for commonalities. I call these ***Intersections of Opportunity***—the overlaps between what you are after and what others seek. The first superpower of being able to galvanize people into a better future is to start from where you overlap on what that future looks like. These are by far the easiest ways to configure with others to build a better future situation.

But it's not the only way. If you don't overlap with someone, it doesn't mean you can't lead-follow your way into a future with them. While not as easy to attract people into, you can barter with your desired futures. Simplistically, it might sound a bit like, "If you help me produce this outcome I care about, I will help you produce the one you care about." Many times, we find ourselves in these. For example, "You do this work I need for me, and I will pay you enough to do what you want." It's acceptable to produce incremental leadership—it doesn't always have to be inspired leadership. Maybe they won't write books about it, but a better future produced together is still a better future for both of you.

Stewards of the Future

I sat in a business conference one morning and listened as the speaker asked people to raise their hand if they would rather lead than follow. Most all the hands went up. Mine didn't. I help lead teams across three enterprises, yet I am quite clear that I will happily follow anyone who has the better thinking for how to produce the future we want together. Great thinking can come from anyone. I stand ready to follow. Best as I can tell, none of us gets to be "the leader." Rather, we get to be stewards of a better future together. Sometimes that means I need to lead, sometimes that means I need to follow.

Let's break past all the platitudes of leadership and recognize it for what it is: one hand clapping. Great leadership is defined more by the excellence of the followership they attract to work with them, as by their individual acts of leadership. Many of the greatest advances I have made in career and business came when I checked my ego at the door, heard the better interpretation from someone else, and stood ready to follow. I encourage all who consider themselves as leaders or aspiring to lead to really see themselves as working to master the skills of leadership-followership, or followership-leadership. Let's not focus exclusively on the societal impulse to imbue supposed leadership characteristics. Instead, let's focus on producing a better future together than we ever could have apart, and let the roles land where they create the best likelihood for success towards that future.

EPILOGUE

Now that you've had a chance to learn about luminary leadership from some of those who know most about the subject, how do you feel about it yourself? Do you feel that you can use some of the principles and techniques you've learned from the book in your own work as a leader? Have you read about any new strategies and tactics for being a leader that appear relevant to what you do day-to-day?

Luminary Leadership offers a plethora of advice on what it takes to be an impactful—perhaps even great—leader. And while some of the leadership strategies or techniques mentioned in the book were covered by multiple authors, it was often with such a fresh twist or perspective that it felt to me like I was treading on new ground in each chapter. The following are what struck me as some of the book's main takeaways:

Learn to Be a Leader

Luminary leaders, or any leaders, are more made than born. While there may be some core skills that could help one be a leader, the greatest portion of a leader's skill is learned through training and experience gained in the field. Whether that training comes from a mentor or reading a book on leadership, the key, according to many of the authors, is not only to dedicate significant time and effort to the learning process but also to become a lifelong learner. Luminary leaders typically learn from any source available to them, including education and training, informal or otherwise, and experience. To truly excel as a leader, learning as much as you can as often (and as long) as you can is crucial.

A Leader Needs Values and Vision

It's hard to inspire people unless you strongly believe in and follow your values, and those values resonate with your team. From honesty to helping others to hard work and being willing to do yourself what you ask your people to do, the values of a leader are vital to establishing their leadership style and enabling their team to understand what is expected of them and what they can expect of you as a leader.

A leader's vision, often closely linked to their values, is cited by many of the authors as an absolutely essential part of being a luminary leader. To gain the buy-in, you need to inspire your team to work at its best. It is vital not only to have a vision but also to communicate it clearly. To the degree possible, your vision should be designed with feedback from your team. If they have had a chance to weigh in, it can increase the team's dedication to seeing it come to fruition.

The Traits of a Leader

The leadership traits enumerated in the book paint a detailed picture of what differentiates a leader. These behaviors serve as the fuel that enables leaders to develop and present a vision that resonates with their people and to bounce back from failure when it occurs. Organization is an important trait for leaders, as is belief in yourself, and the courage to take chances when appropriate.

Motivating people is another key trait of a leader, as is avoiding the trap of simply managing rather than leading. Leaders need to be adaptive, altering their approach when necessary to achieve their goals. It's also important in this era to become digitally savvy, given the importance of computer technology and online efforts in modern business.

Delegating responsibilities is another important trait of a luminary leader—nobody can know or do everything themselves and learning to hand off tasks to your team is crucial to optimizing your leadership ability. Communication is another key skill for a leader, as are self-confidence, problem-solving, and emotional intelligence. Finally, lead with love rather than fear—your team will be much more likely to stick with you and the mission through thick and thin if you do.

How to Motivate People

A big part of what it takes to motivate people is to understand them—what drives them, what they find most enjoyable about the job, what they feel they are best at, what their goals are. Getting to know them not only builds camaraderie but also improves your ability to find the right role for them, which is a motivating factor in and of itself.

Beyond understanding your team members, as mentioned above, communicating your vision and being willing to get into the trenches and work with them when appropriate are also good ways to motivate people. Money alone is often not enough—it's a mistake to think that money is the only thing that motivates people. It is certainly a major factor, but other things can be very important as well: meaningful work, responsibility, respect, the social aspect of the job. For the younger generation in particular, work/life balance is seen as being extremely important for motivational purposes.

Success and Failure to a Luminary Leader

One of the most notable traits attributed to luminary leaders by several authors was their refusal to let failure stop them. Many of these leaders devised strategies to overcome their initial failures or bounced back from a failed company or venture by starting over, from scratch if necessary. Resilience was one of the qualities that set them apart from ordinary leaders. Another quality of luminary leaders that stands out is their ability to treat failures or setbacks as learning experiences. They use them to build on what they have learned, helping them to ultimately achieve their goals, even in the face of seemingly insurmountable obstacles.

Another major element of these leaders' skill sets is their ability to inspire and motivate those around them, both by their personal behavior and the vision they expound and, often, embody by their actions. Luminary leaders understand the value of starting small and aiming for attainable victories early on to build team unity and improve buy-in. Ultimately, such leaders know that winning and success are team efforts. They methodically combine vision, hard work, motivation, and inspiration to build teams that can get the job done, whether that is improving the organization, its people, or its ability to achieve its objectives and realize its mission.